Financial Makeover
Your Guide to Strategic Money Management, Wealth Building, and Debt-Free Living

Derrick C. Porter

Financial Makeover

Copyright Page

Copyright © 2024 by [Derrick C. Porter]. All rights reserved.

Except for brief quotations included in critical reviews and certain other noncommercial uses allowed by copyright law, no part of this publication may be reproduced, distributed, or transmitted in any form or by any means, including photocopying, recording, or other electronic or mechanical methods, without the publisher's prior written permission.

Disclaimer:

This book, which draws on the author's studies and experiences, aims to provide broad knowledge about personal finance. It is not meant to be used as a replacement for counsel from a licensed financial planner or another expert in the field of finance. Everybody has a different financial condition, so what works for one person may not work for another.

The tactics and examples covered here are just meant to serve as examples and do not guarantee the same results. The correctness, application, suitability, and completeness of the information in this book are not warranted or represented by the author or publisher. This book's content is only meant to be used for educational purposes.

You thereby assume complete responsibility for your conduct if you choose to adopt the concepts in this book. No party shall ever hold the author or publisher responsible for any direct, indirect, punitive, special, incidental, or other consequential damages resulting from the use of this content, whether directly or indirectly.

About The Author

Derrick C. Porter is a respected financial counselor, author, and speaker who is well-known for his practical approach to wealth management and personal finance. With more than twenty years of expertise in the financial sector, Derrick has devoted his professional life to helping people reach financial stability and independence.

Childhood and Schooling
Derrick was raised in a middle-class home where hard work and education were prized. He pursued a finance degree at a top institution since he was always interested in numbers and the idea of managing money. He excelled academically and had a strong interest in economic theory, investments, and personal finance.

Career
Following his graduation, Derrick began working for a reputable financial planning company, where his creative

thinking and commitment to customer success allowed him to advance fast through the ranks. Seeing a need in the industry for useful, approachable financial guidance, he struck out on his own to create a financial consulting company that specialized in offering individualized financial planning services.

Composing and Delivering Public Addresses

Derrick wrote "Financial Makeover" because he wanted to touch more people and reach a larger audience. His years of knowledge and wisdom are condensed into a thorough manual that is intended to assist readers in navigating the challenges of personal finance.

In addition to being a writer, Derrick gives popular speeches. He makes a lot of trips, giving keynote addresses, workshops, and seminars at conferences to spread his message of resilience and financial freedom. Many guests find him to be very engaging and empathic, which motivates them to start the process of being financially independent.

Personal Life and Philanthropy

Beyond his career pursuits, Derrick has a strong commitment to charity, especially with regard to financial literacy and education initiatives for impoverished areas. He thinks it's important to give back to the community and support projects that provide people the resources they need to achieve financial success.

In his own time, Derrick likes to travel, explore the outdoors, and keep learning about the always changing financial and investing landscape. He is a lifelong student who is always looking for fresh insights and opportunities to improve both his career and quality of life.

Historical and Upcoming Initiatives

The enduring dedication of Derrick C. Porter to financial empowerment and education defines his legacy. Looking forward, he intends to go on writing and giving speeches, and he has a number of new initiatives in the works that will further streamline financial planning and make financial health available to everyone.

Through his work in general and his book "Financial Makeover," Derrick personifies the idea that anybody who is prepared to study, make plans, and strive toward their financial objectives can achieve financial independence.

Financial Makeover

Table of Contents

Copyright Page...2
About The Author..4
Table of Contents..8
Introduction: **Welcome to Your Financial Makeover Journey**..10
    Realizing How Important It Is to Take Charge of Your Money... 12
Chapter One: Assessing Your Financial Situation.. 16
A: Identifying Your Current Financial Status................ 16
B: Analyzing Your Income and Expenses......................22
C: Evaluating Your Debts and Liabilities.......................28
Chapter Two: Setting Clear Financial Goals............ 36
A: What Are Goals?... 36
B. Prioritizing Your Financial Objectives.......................42
C. Creating a Realistic and Achievable Action Plan..... 49
Chapter Three: Creating a Solid Financial Foundation..56
A. Personal Budget...56
B. Building an Emergency Fund: Protecting Yourself Against Financial Setbacks...61
C. Managing Debt: Techniques for Effective Debt Repayment... 72
Chapter Four: Implementing Smart Money Management Techniques..84

A. Saving and Investing: Growing Your Wealth Over Time..84
B. Making Well-Informed Financial Decisions: Steering Clear of Common Money Errors................................ 101
C. Common Financial Mistakes To Avoid................... 104

Chapter Five: Overcoming Financial Challenges.. 114
A. Dealing with Unexpected Expenses and Financial Emergencies... 114
B. Handling Financial Setbacks: Strategies for Bouncing Back Stronger... 120
C. Building Resilience: Cultivating a Positive Money Mindset... 125

Chapter Six: Maintaining Financial Wellness.........132
A. Monitoring Your Progress: Tracking Your Financial Goals... 132
B. Adjusting Your Financial Plan as Needed.............. 138
C. Milestone Celebration: Honoring Your Successes Along the Way.. 141

Chapter Seven: Living a Fulfilling Generous Life.144
A. Enjoying the Fruits of Your Financial Makeover: Living Debt-free and Stress-free... 144
B. Giving Back: Using Your Financial Resources to Make a Positive Impact... 147
C. Money Myths You Should Disbelieve Right Now... 150

Conclusion.. 158
Request for a Review... 162
References.. 164

Introduction

Welcome to Your Financial Makeover Journey

Sincerely, I'm thrilled to have you here as we prepare to start this life-changing path toward wealth and financial independence. It's a trip that revolves on you, your objectives, your aspirations, and your own route to financial prosperity.

Let's begin by admitting something crucial: managing your money might seem like a daunting task. Feeling that way is OK. The fact is, however, that just by being here, you have already made the first step. And believe me, that's a tremendous feat.

I want you to know that as we embark on this adventure together, I'm not here to lecture you or confuse you with technical financial terms. No, my objective is to be your largest supporter, collaborator, and mentor during the whole process.

Financial Makeover

So fasten your seatbelts, for we have a lot of terrain to cover. We'll begin by carefully examining your present financial circumstances. We'll examine your earnings, outlays, obligations, and savings to get a comprehensive understanding of your situation.

We'll then establish some objectives, both large and little, and everything in between. Do you want to settle your school debt? Amass money for a down payment on a property? Put money aside for retirement now? Whatever your objectives are, we'll work together to create a strategy that will make them a reality.

I won't lie to you now—there could be some difficulties along the road. Unexpected costs, tempting last-minute purchases, and maybe even a few disappointments. The good news is that every hurdle on the way is an opportunity to learn and grow.

My aim of writing this book above all, is to encourage you, provide guidance and useful strategies that will help you get through any challenge you may encounter. Together, we'll confidently and tenaciously negotiate the ups and downs of your financial path.

Hey, it's not all that serious. We'll commemorate all of your victories, large and little, along the path. Settled a credit card debt? Give yourself a special meal. Saved up to a significant amount? It could be time for a weekend trip. Recall that the trip is just as much about having fun along the way as it is about arriving at your objective.

So settle down on your comfortable seat, fill a cup with your preferred beverage, and get ready to go off on an incredible journey.

Realizing How Important It Is to Take Charge of Your Money

It's time to discuss about managing your money. I realize this isn't the most glamorous subject, but believe me when I say that it's one of the most self-empowering things you can do.

The truth is that you have power over your future when you manage your funds. It goes beyond just having enough cash on hand to cover expenses (though that certainly plays a role). It's about being able to live your life as you see fit—to follow your interests, achieve your goals, and persevere through any challenges that may arise.

Just think about it: it's difficult to concentrate on anything else when you're always worried about money.

Every unanticipated cost seems like a kick in the stomach, and every statement you get in the mail serves as a constant reminder of how unstable your finances really are.

Life does not have to be that way. You can end the cycle of worry and uncertainty and begin creating the life you've always desired by taking charge of your finances.

What does it really mean to manage your finances? Well, organizing yourself is the first step. Make a list of all of your costs, debts, savings, and income. Obtain a thorough understanding of your situation so that you may decide where you want to go.

It's all about goal-setting after that. With your money, what goals do you want to accomplish? Perhaps your goals are to start saving for retirement, pay off your school debts, or save money for a down payment on a home. Whatever your objectives are, put them in writing, divide them into more manageable chunks, and go to work.

The problem is that defining objectives is just the first stage. In order to go from where you are to where you want to be, you also need a plan—a road map. This entails making sure every dollar has a purpose, monitoring your expenditure, and developing a budget.

The truth is that managing money isn't always simple. It requires self-control, endurance, and sometimes a little amount of sacrifice. The problem is, though: it's worthwhile. Because you have power over your future when you manage your funds. And it's difficult to stop that sensation. So prepare to take charge of your money by taking a deep breath, rolling up your sleeves, and getting started. You won't regret it, I promise.

Financial Makeover

Chapter One

Assessing Your Financial Situation

A: Identifying Your Current Financial Status

One of the first steps in getting your financial house in order is taking stock of where you are financially right now. I realize it sounds scary, but I assure you, it's really not. If you want to know your exact financial situation, what does it mean? Well, it boils down to honestly assessing your current financial situation. Just like taking a picture of your financial situation, this will help you identify what's working, what isn't, and where you should make adjustments. Getting into complex financial statements or pulling out a plethora of fancy spreadsheets is not what I mean here. No, we're aiming for a no-frills approach here.

You must have an accurate picture of your present financial status before you can take any significant steps toward monetary stability and credit score improvement. Doing so requires tallying up your money coming in and going out, as well as your assets and debts. For you to identify areas that you need to improve on, and as well make quality decisions about your financial goals, you must assess your financial situation thoroughly. For a detailed analysis of your present financial status, follow these steps:

1. Gather Financial records: Start by collecting together all your financial records, including bank accounts, credit card statements, loan statements, pay stubs, and any other documents that give insight into your income, spending, and obligations.

2. Calculate Your Income:Next, it's time to take a big breath and plunge in. Start by looking at your income. How much do you bring in every month? Determine your monthly income by summing up all sources of revenue, including salary, bonuses, freelance work, rental income, and any other sources. Are you getting a stable salary, or is your income more variable?

3. Identify Your Fixed costs: Fixed costs are recurrent expenses that are largely consistent from month to month. Once you've got a grasp on your revenue, it's time to shift your focus to your spending. What are you spending your money on each month? Start by writing down all your normal expenses—things like rent or mortgage payments, utilities, food, and transportation expenditures. Then, take a look at your discretionary spending—are there places where you might cut down a bit?

4. Track Your Variable costs: Variable costs are expenses that might change from month to month, such as groceries, eating out, entertainment, and discretionary spending. To monitor your variable costs, analyze your bank and credit card accounts for the preceding several months and classify your spending. This can help you find places where you may possibly cut down and save money.

5. compute Your Debt-to-Income ratio: Your debt-to-income ratio (DTI) is a critical indicator that

Financial Makeover

lenders use to evaluate your capacity to handle debt. It estimates the proportion of your income that goes towards debt repayment. DTI equals your total monthly debt payment, divided by your gross monthly income, multiplied by 100. Ideally, your DTI should be around 36%, with lower percentages suggesting greater financial health.

6. Evaluate Your valuables and Liabilities: Make a list of all of your valued items, including real estate, investments, savings accounts, and other valuables. List all of your obligations at the same time, including any unpaid credit card debt, outstanding loans, and other commitments. This can assist you in determining your net worth and point out any areas in which you may be able to improve.

7. Set Financial objectives: Establish attainable and reasonable financial objectives based on your evaluation of your existing financial status. These objectives can be debt repayment, emergency fund accumulation, retirement savings, or future investment. By setting specific objectives, you'll provide yourself a financial balance and raise your credit score.

8. Savings: Last but not least, remember to check your savings. How much cash do you keep in reserve for a rainy day? Do you have money put up for emergencies? If not, that's OK; together, we'll endeavor to construct one. You will learn a lot about your income, spending, obligations, and assets by taking a close look at your present financial status. This will give you the needed information that will guide you in deciding your financial goals and provide the foundation for building a strong credit score.

After putting all of this information on paper, stand back and consider the larger picture. What emotions does it arouse? Do you think things might be done better, or are you content with where you are now? Recall that determining your present financial situation is just the beginning of your path to financial independence. But it's a crucial one, I assure you. Thus, be patient, honest with yourself, and prepared to take charge of your financial situation. This is something you can handle!

Real Life Practical Example

Let's look at Chloe's actual circumstances. She just graduated from college and is just beginning her job. Chloe is thrilled to be starting to make money now that she has her first job. She is, meanwhile, also experiencing some overwhelm due to her financial circumstances. She is aware that she needs to manage her money better, but she is unsure of where to begin.

Chloe makes the decision to examine her income, spending, obligations, and savings in more detail in order to determine her present financial situation.

Income: To calculate her monthly income, Chloe compiles her most current pay stubs. She determines her take-home income after deducting all applicable taxes and other costs.

Expenses: She then keeps tabs on her monthly outlays. To find out where her money is going, she looks over her credit card bills and bank statements. She breaks down her spending into areas such as utilities, food, rent, entertainment, and eating out.

Debts: Chloe tallies her outstanding loans. She enumerates all of her outstanding credit card bills, school loan amounts, and any debts that she may have accrued. She lists each debt's total amount outstanding along with the required minimum payment each month.

Savings: Lastly, Chloe verifies the amount in her savings account. She checks the amount of money she has set aside for unforeseen costs and emergencies. She also takes into consideration the existence of any retirement savings accounts, such as an IRA or 401(k).

Having gone through this procedure, Chloe's financial condition is now more apparent. Even while her income is consistent, she discovers that her expenses—particularly for entertainment and eating out—are more than she had budgeted for. She also finds out that she has relatively little saved and a large amount of debt from education loans.

Now that she has this knowledge, Chloe is able to make wise financial choices. She may make a plan to pay off her debts, identify areas where she needs to make spending reductions, and begin setting aside money for emergencies and future objectives. Chloe has started down the path to financial success and stability by taking the time to assess her present financial situation.

B: Analyzing Your Income and Expenses

Analyzing your income and spending is a crucial step towards taking control of your money, so let's talk about it. Doesn't that sound a little intimidating? You need not fear; I will simplify and make things easier to comprehend for you.

Let's start by talking about Income:
Income is the amount received or earned within a certain time frame. Your monthly income is the total amount of money you earn from all sources combined, including

side jobs, your work, and other sources within the month. Examine your invoices, pay stubs, and any other financial records that you may have. Your income is the total of all of the above. Because there are many methods to generate money, there are different labels for it. Wages or salaries are the income derived from job or self-employment. Similar to savings accounts, interest on deposit accounts may also be derived via lending. A shareholder who owns stock is entitled to any dividends that are paid out. One is entitled to a draw if they own stock in a privately owned company or partnership.

In a market-based economy, selling labor or selling capital are the two main methods to make money. Selling labor entails working for oneself or for another. Paychecks are the source of income. Other benefits like life insurance, health insurance, or retirement contributions may be included in total remuneration. In the labor market, labor is sold. Selling capital entails investing, which is taking extra money and giving it to a person in need of liquidity (access to cash) via sales or rentals. Lending is the capital rented out; the rent is the interest. Lending may be done via a public debt market by purchasing business, government, or government agency bonds, or it can be done privately through a direct agreement with a borrower. Purchasing or investing in corporate stock is one way to trade funds for a portion of the future worth of the business.

Several additional assets are available for investment, including land, coins, art, antiques, and commodities including light crude oil, platinum, live animals, soybeans, and cattle. The idea behind investment is the same: investing is renting cash or selling it for an item that has the potential to generate income in the future, be resold later, or both. Similar to how the dairy department is a distinct area of the supermarket, capital is sold in the capital market and loaned in the credit market.

Let's move on to the expenses:

Expenses are the price paid for goods or resources that are used up or used on a daily basis. Expenses are the monthly costs you incur, such as rent, food, bills, and all those little extras that rapidly mount up. Make a note of every cost you incur each month to start. Remember the little pleasures in life, like your favorite streaming service or your daily cup of coffee. Due to the daily depletion of resources like food, shelter, clothes, energy, and so on, expenses are recurrent, meaning they occur again.

You have a budget deficit when your income is less than your spending because you don't have enough money to meet your requirements and goals. A budget deficit is not fiscally feasible and cannot be sustained. There are just three options left: either cut costs, raise revenue, or borrow the difference to close the deficit. Although borrowing can seem like the simplest and fastest option, it actually raises costs since it adds interest to the mix. Borrowing to make up for a deficit will only make it worse unless revenue can be boosted as well. The best options are to raise income or cut costs, but these are often more difficult to do.

After you've made your list, you should delve a bit more. Examine every cost and consider whether you really need it or if you could live without it. Perhaps you're paying for subscriptions you don't actually use, or you've discovered you're spending more money on eating out than you thought. This is your opportunity to find any places where you can make savings and minimize costs.

Let's do some math now. You can calculate how much you spend each month by adding up all of your costs. Subtract that amount from your income after that. What remains? This is your income that you may spend as you like, once your essential costs have been paid. You can see clearly where your money is going and where you may be able to make some adjustments by analyzing your revenue and spending. It's all about being mindful of your spending habits and finding ways to make your money work harder for you.

Real Life Practical Example

Going back to Chloe s case, let's take a closer look at her earnings and outlays:

Let's begin with earnings. For Chloe, who just graduated from college and is just beginning her career, her work provides the majority of her income. She receives a salary of $45,000 per year, or around $3,750 monthly before taxes.

This is when the intriguing part begins: After paying her bills, Chloe expected to have more money, but it seems that her costs are taking up a significant portion of her earnings. So let's examine her spending in more detail. Chloe begins by classifying them as follows:

Housing: She pays $1,200 a month in rent, which also covers her utilities (electricity and water).

Transit: Her monthly petrol expenditure for her automobile is $100, and she also spends an additional $100 on public transit to go to work.

Food: Every month, Chloe sets aside $300 for food and another $200 for going out to eat and getting coffee with friends.

Services & Utilities: Chloe spends around $100 a month for her phone and internet services in addition to her housing.

Health & Well-Being: She pays $50 a month for a gym membership.

Entertainment: Since Chloe enjoys relaxing after work, she sets aside $100 a month for hobbies, concerts, and movies.

Miscellaneous: Unexpected costs like toiletries, clothes, and presents constantly come up. Chloe sets aside $100 a month for these sporadic expenses.

Chloe finds that, after adding up all of her costs, her monthly spending comes to $2,150. She is left with $1,600 per month after deducting this from her $3,750 monthly salary. $1,600 can seem to be a reasonable sum of money to have after paying bills at first sight. However, Chloe finds out that she has to be more deliberate about where she's spending that additional money after looking more closely at her financial objectives, which include paying off her college debts and setting aside money for the future.

She gets a better idea of her financial status by looking at her income and spending. She can see where her money is going, where she can make savings, and where she can put more money down to accomplish her goals. It's an effective tool that gives her the ability to manage her money and make more informed financial choices.

Recall that keeping track of your earnings and outlays isn't about denying yourself the things you want to do; rather, it's about ensuring that your money is working as hard as it can for you. Thus, take the time to run the numbers, assess your situation, and begin taking action to improve your financial future. This is something you can handle!

C: Evaluating Your Debts and Liabilities

Liabilities and debt are concepts that we are all quite acquainted with. It is essential to comprehend these two terms in their entirety if you want to better your financial situation and reach complete financial independence. Liability and debt may first seem to signify the same thing, but they are not the same. All debts are liabilities but not all liabilities are considered as debts, to put it simply, liabilities are any outstanding financial obligations, while debt is expressly defined as money borrowed.

Debt: What is It?

Debt is the total amount of money borrowed from a person, business, or institution. The interest is the portion of the agreement that must be paid back in order for the debt to be settled. Different people and organizations have different repayment plans for their debts. Known by its constant name, interest, this fee is always expressed as a percentage of the principal amount received.

In the event that you manage a firm, debt is always detrimental since it gives other parties the right to benefit from your venture. Paying close attention to the specifics is always advised while using a credit card, business line of credit, or any other kind of credit, so that you can keep an eye on the interest that is accruing on your debt.

It's important to note that if you borrow money to expand your capital structure, debt may actually help your business. If you pay off your debt quickly and with good management, it may enhance cash flow and provide a chance for your company to accumulate cash reserves.

What actions can you take to get financial independence and pay off debt?

•Reduce spending

You must limit your spending if you want to lower your debt. Living a debt-free life is easier when you spend less money. Review your budget to discover where you may make savings by looking at your present outlays. These costs cover the purchase of any unnecessary extravagance, such as several homes or a new automobile. You have a better chance of enjoying a debt-free life the less you spend.

•Make a second career
Establishing a second source of income or taking a job is one of the finest strategies to pay off your debt. By choosing a part-time job, you may generate additional revenue. If you are skilled in a certain area, for example, you may work a part-time job in that industry. You will be able to pay off your debt more quickly as a result of this increase in your income.

•Make use of your resources
Making additional money from your asset might be another helpful method for paying off your debts. For example, if you own your own home and are the only occupant, you may want to think about renting out a portion of the space. Although choosing this choice will make things less convenient for you, keep in mind that this is only a temporary situation. You may get your comfort back after paying off your debts. You could think about living with your parents, relatives, or friends if you don't have a place of your own. This will assist

you in lowering the amount of rent or other fees you pay each month for a room or a home.

•Speak with your creditor.
Everyone can pay off their bills in flawless fashion, but not everyone is aware of this tactic. In your debt repayment arrangement, your creditor may give you some leeway. Did you know this? They certainly can! You may get in touch with your creditor and renegotiate the conditions of your agreement if you want to enhance your debt records. The IVA is one of the strongest debt methods available today, and it may be used for a wide range of obligations.

Liabilities
Liabilities are defined as your commitments, debts, and those that need financial input from you. Liabilities are often understood to be things that diminish something's worth or anything of value, such as money, tranquility, pleasure, security, or confidence. Something that undermines your mental and financial strength, something that keeps you from reaching your objectives, something that causes negative stress, strain, and anxiety, something that impairs your productivity and health. Generally speaking, anything that depletes you is a liability, and everything that strengthens you is an asset.

What doable actions can you take to reduce your liabilities?

•Sell any unused assets

Selling old and superfluous assets is one of the finest strategies to lower your responsibilities. Redundant assets include extra cars, old equipment, etc. You may immediately lower your obligations by getting rid of any unnecessary assets.

• Personal Stock Taking

You may make a personal inventory of everything you possess to reduce your obligations. Examine your possessions and determine which ones cost you money. You may not be able to recognize what depletes your finances unless you take stock of all that you do with money.

•Transform your debts into assets

How can I turn my obligations into assets, you may wonder? Selling a liability and using the proceeds to fund an existing company or launch a new one is one of the easiest methods to do this. Consider selling whatever assets you have, for example, in order to launch a company.

Real Life Practical Example

Let's dive into Chloe's journey to better understand how evaluating debts and liabilities can be a game-changer in managing personal finances.

Chloe, like many of us, found herself juggling a few financial plates—student loans, a credit card balance, and a car loan. It felt like every month was a tightrope walk over a canyon of bills. She knew it was time for a change, to get her finances under control and stop feeling like her paycheck was disappearing into thin air.

Breaking Down the Debt

The first step Chloe took was to list all her debts. She created a simple table that included her student loans ($25,000 at 6% interest), her credit card debt ($3,500 at 19% interest), and her car loan ($10,000 at 5% interest). Next to each, she wrote down the minimum monthly payment and the interest rate.

Understanding the Impact

Chloe realized that not all debts are created equal. Her credit card debt, though not the largest amount, had the highest interest rate. This meant she was paying more over time just for the privilege of owing money. The student loans, despite being a larger sum, had a relatively lower interest rate and offered more flexible repayment options.

Setting Priorities
Knowing she couldn't tackle everything at once, Chloe decided to prioritize her debts. She chose to focus on the credit card debt first because the high interest rate was a big drain on her resources. She decided to make more than the minimum payment on this debt each month, while still meeting the minimum payments on her student loans and car loan.

Making a Plan
To free up extra money for her credit card debt, Chloe looked for areas where she could cut back on spending. She started bringing lunch to work instead of eating out, canceled a few subscription services she rarely used, and set a stricter budget for her leisure activities. Every dollar she saved went straight to paying down her credit card debt.

Seeing the Progress
Every month, Chloe took a few minutes to review her debts and track her progress. It was incredibly motivating to see the numbers go down. As her credit card debt decreased, she found she was paying less in interest each month, which only accelerated her progress.

The Ripple Effect
With her credit card debt finally cleared, Chloe felt a huge weight lifted off her shoulders. She then turned her attention to her car loan, applying the same strategy. The student loans were next. With each debt cleared, she had more money available to tackle the next one, creating a positive snowball effect.

The Takeaway
For Chloe, evaluating her debts and liabilities wasn't just about crunching numbers; it was about taking control of her financial destiny. It showed her the power of prioritizing high-interest debts and the importance of a consistent repayment strategy. Most importantly, it taught her that with determination and a solid plan, climbing out of debt wasn't just possible—it was achievable. Chloe's story is a testament to the fact that, while debt can feel overwhelming, there's always a way out. It starts with understanding what you owe, making a plan to tackle it, and taking things one step at a time.

Chapter Two

Setting Clear Financial Goals

A: What Are Goals?

A "goal" is essentially a result, an ambition, or a desire that you want to accomplish. For instance, achieving a marathon, cutting a few post-Christmas pounds, or raising money. The problem is that these goals are really just wishes or fantasies until you put them in writing and provide yourself with a schedule and a plan for achieving them.

There are two types of life objectives: long-term goals and short-term goals. Both are necessary for total success. To be honest, however, there are moments when the time and effort required to accomplish long-term objectives might seem excessive. This is where short-term objectives are useful!

Short-term objectives are modest, doable targets. These "everyday goals" are what get you closer to your final objective. It's easy to lose steam while pursuing bigger objectives that seem so far off. Short-term objectives are easy victories that you can accomplish in a shorter amount of time.

Short-term objectives, as their name suggests, are great for constrained time frames; you'll be astounded at what you can do in a short period of time.

What distinguishes long-term goals from short-term goals?

It would be hard to discuss short-term objectives without also discussing long-term ones. While the two complement each other, they also vary greatly. While long-term objectives usually take significantly longer to achieve, short-term goals are intended to be accomplished in a shorter amount of time.

Long-term objectives are the greatest place to start. Next, as stepping stones to the long-term goals, identify short-term objectives. In this manner, every short-term objective sets up a longer-term objective. One of the essential behaviors of successful individuals is this. This method of goal-setting ensures that you are always moving toward your end objective. Although long-term and short-term objectives often complement each other, there are some clear distinctions between the two. Let's examine each term in more detail.

Short Term Goals

Short-term objectives are similar to the tasks you have right now. These are goals you want to accomplish as quickly as possible, usually in the next year. They serve as the fundamental pieces that provide the groundwork for your loftier goals.

You may establish a short-term savings goal like putting money away for an emergency fund, or you could set a career objective like finishing an enhanced skills course. A short-term aim may also serve as a springboard or practical step toward a longer-term objective. Establish short-term objectives and track your progress to realize those transformative dreams.

Consider yourself someone who is just beginning to grasp the concept of budgeting. A short-term objective may be to save a certain amount of money every month by eating out less and using fewer subscription services. It's specific, measurable, and attainable in a timely manner, providing you with a feeling of satisfaction and a little victory for your financial well-being.

Short-Term Goals (Less than one year)					
Priority	Goal	Total Cost	Duration	Monthly Cost	Target Date

Long-Term Goal:

A long-term goal is something you want to accomplish someday, but it will need patience, time, and preparation. You could need 10 years to finish them; you can't just dust them off in a few weeks. As these objectives often include many smaller objectives or stages, it's critical to establish short-term objectives in addition to your long-term strategy. Your long-term objective can be to start your own company, save money for your retirement account, etc. See how each one provides you with a feeling of purpose and direction in life, much like a huge goal or long-term vision? Yes, long-term objectives might sometimes appear daunting or even unachievable. But you will ultimately succeed if you follow through on each short-term objective you set for yourself along the road.

Long-Term Goals (Over ten years)					
Priority	Goal	Total Cost	Duration	Monthly Cost	Target Date

Realistic Example: Retiring comfortably is a common long-term objective. Many minor actions are involved in achieving this objective, such as setting aside a certain portion of your salary every year, making prudent investments, and controlling your expenditure over a long period of time. It's the type of objective you strive for for a good deal of your life, and it influences a lot of your financial choices along the way.

When you need a goal that falls somewhere between short- and long-term objectives, you might consider a medium-term, intermediate, or mid-term goal. Although you can often accomplish medium-term objectives in less than five years, this might vary from goal to goal and person to person.

Mid-Term Goals

The next steps up the staircase are known as mid-term objectives. You want to accomplish these objectives during the next two to five years. Though they need a little more forethought and perseverance than short-term objectives, they are essential building blocks for your larger vision.

As an example, let's pretend you've succeeded in saving $200 a month, your short-term target. You may now decide to save money for a new car's down payment as a mid-term objective. If the automobile you desire needs a $10,000 down payment, you would need to save steadily at your present pace for around 4 years. Though more difficult than short-term objectives, it is totally doable with dedication and a well-thought-out strategy.

Creating a life roadmap is made easier when you set objectives in these three areas. Your long-term objectives keep your eyes on the target, your mid-term goals give you momentum, and your short-term goals get you started. It's about taking little, significant steps at a time, and striking a balance between present demands and future goals. Whether your aim is to purchase a vehicle, save for a rainy day fund, or prepare for retirement, each one is essential to creating the life you want to lead.

Mid-Term Goals (1-10 years)					
Priority	Goal	Total Cost	Duration	Monthly Cost	Target Date

B. Prioritizing Your Financial Objectives

Prioritizing your financial objectives is a lot like deciding what to pack for a vacation. You can't take everything, so you choose what's most important based on where you're going, what you'll be doing, and what you need most. In finance, this means deciding which goals to focus on first, balancing what you need now

with what you'll need in the future. Let's break this down with some straightforward, practical examples to make it clearer.

1. Identifying Your Goals
First, lay out all your financial goals.
Think of it as laying out everything you want to pack for that trip. You've got short-term goals (like saving for a holiday), mid-term goals (like buying a car), and long-term goals (like retirement savings).

Practical Example: Philip and Emilia sit down and write out everything they want to achieve financially. They list everything from paying off credit card debt, saving for a trip to Japan, buying a new car, renovating their kitchen, and putting away money for retirement.

2. Assessing Your Resources
Next, figure out how much you can "pack." This means taking a good look at your income, your expenses, and seeing how much you have left to allocate towards your goals after you've covered the essentials.

Practical Example: Philip and Emilia calculate they have $500 a month they can divide among their goals after all their essential expenses are covered.

3. Prioritizing Based on Urgency and Importance
Now, decide what needs to go in your "suitcase" first. What's urgent? What's important? And what can wait? Urgent goals are usually those that have a time constraint or are critical for your financial stability (like paying off high-interest debt). Important goals are necessary for your long-term well-being (like retirement savings).

Practical Example: Philip and Emilia decide paying off their $2,000 credit card debt is urgent because of the high interest. They consider the trip to Japan important but not urgent, so they decide to tackle the debt first, then start saving for the trip. The car purchase can wait a bit, and they decide to contribute a small amount towards their retirement regularly, no matter what.

4. Establishing a Schedule
Give each of your priority goals a reasonable timeframe. Considering your monthly contribution, how long would it take you to reach each goal?

Useful Example: They determine that if they set aside $500 each month, they can pay off their credit card debt

in around four months. They anticipate needing another year to save enough money for the trip to Japan, so they want to save the same amount after that.

5. Periodically Evaluate Your Strategy
Your objectives and financial status may change. To make necessary adjustments to your strategy, you must check in often.

Real-World Example: Philip receives a raise after six months. They choose to divide the additional income between their retirement savings and their Japan vacation fund, perhaps advancing both their long-term investment and trip at the same time.

Setting financial goals in order of importance may first seem daunting, but you can make a plan that works for you by dissecting the process into manageable, unambiguous stages. Recall that the key is to make calculated decisions, exercise flexibility, and focus on the end goal, which might be debt relief, a luxurious trip, or a happy retirement.

Setting priorities for your finances will enable you to pursue them more successfully. To achieve your desired success, you need to decide which of the following categories each of your goals belongs to:

Necessary Goals: It is imperative that you don't put off important objectives like setting up an emergency fund, saving for retirement, and being ready to pay for growing healthcare expenditures as you become older.

Significant Goals: While less crucial, important aims still embody fundamental principles. These might include paying for schooling, accumulating savings for a house, reducing debt, or leaving a legacy.

Aspirational Goals: Aspirational objectives go at the bottom of your priority list since they are just nice-to-have items, like a second house or a major vacation.

Establishing whether your objectives are short- or long-term, as well as whether they are necessary, significant, or aspirational, can help you create a strategy for carefully and purposefully investing your resources.

Here are four essential rules to help you manage your short- and long-term financial objectives and prioritize your savings. 1) Establish a spending plan. 2) Create an emergency fund and then give long-term objectives priority. 3) Set aside money for immediate needs. 4) Increase your savings and practice fiscal restraint.

1. Establish a spending plan
You must first determine your monthly spending in order to determine how much you can save:

After accounting for any voluntary contributions you may already be making to a retirement plan, determine your net income. Make a note of everything you spend money on, including recurring but non-monthly costs and monthly purchases made with cash and credit cards. Next, group the figures according to categories, such as grocery, utilities, healthcare, and entertainment. To find out how much money you have left over for savings, now compare your net income to your total costs.

2. Create an emergency fund and rank your long-term objectives first.
The emergency fund comes first: It's common advice from financial gurus to save aside enough cash for three to six months' worth of living costs. Generally speaking, retirement savings should be your next focus. This may even trump a child's college savings account. There is nothing like a student loan or financial help for retirees, yet funding your retirement may be the largest expenditure of your life. Make sure you contribute

enough to get the full match if your employer matches some of your contributions to a retirement plan, such as a 401(k), and your employer provides such a plan.

Employer matching is like receiving a bonus or free money. Take advantage of it!

If you can save more and make enough contributions to get the full company match, you may want to explore funding an Individual Retirement Account (IRA), which is a tax-advantaged retirement account that you open on your own. You may give investing for your children's education top priority after taking care of your retirement savings. A 529 Plan, a Coverdell school Savings Account, or a Custodial Account are just a few of the ways you may invest and save for future school expenses and perhaps get tax savings.

3. Set aside money for immediate needs.
What is considered a brief term? A new house, a wedding, a trip, home renovations, big-ticket goods like vehicles, and comparable acquisitions could be included. Start by listing the things you want to accomplish as a family and yourself during the next five years. After that, order them by importance. For your short-term goals, you might create a savings or investing account, or you could create a different sub account for each target. Then, use whatever extra cash you can set up for savings

to make weekly or monthly contributions. For this reason, a savings account is a viable option since it

provides the possibility of short-term interest returns that are larger.

4. Work on increasing your savings and staying within your means.

Naturally, your unique situation will determine how much you can save, but setting a goal, say 10% to 20% of your income, will assist. If your spending is too high for you to make significant savings, consider ways to reduce the amount of luxury and non-essential purchases. Creating homemade meals, locating free entertainment, increasing the energy efficiency of your house, and many other suggestions are included. Create periodic transfers to your savings and investment accounts to automate your savings. You may be less likely to spend the money if it is sent directly into your savings accounts before you see it.

C. Creating a Realistic and Achievable Action Plan

A detailed set of actions to accomplish a certain objective is called an action plan. It may be seen as a suggested plan for carrying out a certain project in order to successfully and economically accomplish a particular or broad aim. It provides action items and aids in maintaining organization and concentration in both

personal and professional contexts. Tracking progress and maintaining motivation are made simpler by breaking the objective down into smaller, more doable tasks. It's a crucial step in the strategic planning process and enhances collaborative planning. Action plans are useful not only for project management but also for people who want to create a plan to accomplish personal objectives.

An action plan's constituents include:
• Clearly stated objectives;
• Steps and tasks that must be performed in order to accomplish the goal;
• Individuals responsible for completing each task;
• A schedule for task completion that includes deadlines and milestones;
• Tools required to do the assignments; and
• Ways to assess your progress

Advantages of An Action Plan:
• It provides you with a precise path. You will know precisely what has to be done since an action plan outlines the specific tasks to be performed and when they should be finished.

- Writing down and breaking down your objectives into manageable chunks can help you remain inspired and dedicated to the endeavor.

- You can monitor your progress toward your objective with the help of an action plan.
- You can prioritize your tasks based on effort and effect since your action plan outlines every step you need to do.

How Can an Action Plan Be Written?

It seems that making an action plan is not too difficult. To get the most of it, however, there are a few crucial actions you must cautiously take. Here are six simple steps that illustrate how to build an action plan.

Step 1: Identify your ultimate aim

You are setting yourself up for failure if you are unclear about the goals you have for yourself.

Organizing a new project? Establish your current position and your desired destination first.

Resolving an issue? Prioritize the solutions after analyzing the circumstances and looking into potential fixes. Then put your objective in writing.

Additionally, make sure your objective satisfies the SMART criteria before proceeding to the next phase. Alternatively put, ensure that it is. This goal should be:

- Specific—well-defined and unambiguous;

- Measurable—include quantifiable indicators to monitor progress;

- Attainable—realistic and doable given the time, money, expertise, and other resources at your disposal;
- Relevant—align with your other objectives; and
- Timely: includes a completion date

SMART Goal Worksheet

S- Specific	My goal is: eg I want to save $200 every month
M- Measurable	I will track my progress by: eg I will track my progress by logging how much I save monthly on my record sheet
A- Achievable	I will achieve this goal by: eg I will set a reminder on my phone to remind me when to save
R- Relevant	This goal will help me because: eg This goal will help me to save for my rent
T- Time-Bound	I will complete this goal by: eg I will achieve my goal by December 30th.

Step 2: Enumerate the actions that need to be taken.

The objective is evident. How precisely do you go about realizing it?

Make a preliminary template that outlines all the tasks that need to be done, along with the deadlines and individuals accountable. Ensure that every assignment is achievable and has a clear definition. When faced with more complicated and large-scale projects, divide them into smaller, easier-to-manage jobs.

Step 3: Set deadlines and prioritize your work

It's time to prioritize the items on the list and restructure it. Prioritizing certain stages may be necessary since they may be impeding other sub-processes. Include deadlines and make sure they are reasonable. Establish a deadline and work towards it.

Step 4: Establish benchmarks

Milestones may be thought of as little objectives that prepare one for the ultimate major aim. Adding milestones has the benefit of giving you something to look forward to, which keeps you motivated even when the end deadline is far off.

Establish milestones and work your way backwards, starting with the final aim. Don't forget to allow enough time to pass between each milestone you set. Setting milestones two weeks apart is recommended practice.

Step 5: Determine the required resources
Make sure you have all the tools you need on hand to do the chores before you begin working on the project. Additionally, you must first devise a strategy to get them if they are not already accessible. Your budget should be part of this as well. If there are any costs associated with each job, you may designate a column in your action plan to record them.

Step 6: Make your action plan visible
This step's goal is to produce something that can be shared with everyone and that can be quickly understood by everybody. Make sure that your action plan effectively conveys the components we have already established, such as tasks, task owners, deadlines, resources, etc., regardless of whether it is presented as a flowchart, Gantt chart, or table. Everyone should be able to quickly view and amend this document.

Step 7: Monitor, assess, and revise
Set aside some time to assess the advancements you have achieved. On this final action plan, you may

Financial Makeover

highlight your progress toward the target by marking completed activities as done. This will also highlight any

jobs that are unfinished or overdue, in which case you should investigate the cause and come up with workable answers. then make the necessary updates to the action plan.

Chapter Three

Creating a Solid Financial Foundation

A. Personal Budget

A strong grasp of money is crucial in the unpredictable and fast-paced world of today. One of the greatest methods to achieve financial success and stability is to create a personal budget. By closely monitoring their income and spending, anybody can take control of their financial future and make informed choices. But a lot of individuals find budgeting to be a difficult chore, which often results in stress and uncertainty about money.

A key component of financial well-being is personal budgeting, and managing your finances gives you the ability to fulfill your aspirations. Creating a budget gives you a clear view of your earnings and outlays, enabling you to see opportunities for development and make wise financial choices. It offers a path that empowers individuals to take charge of their expenditures, establish financial goals, and make decisions that are reasonable.

Consider John as an example. He just spent the money he got and never cared about it. His inability to adequately plan for paying his rent and other necessary costs caused him to get overwhelmed by the many bills he had to pay as soon as he got his stipends. Making a budget is something that many individuals find difficult, which hinders their capacity to improve financially and leads to a number of practical issues. The following are typical issues that arise from failing to develop personal budgets:

Overspending: If you don't have a budget in place, it's quite easy to overspend and accumulate debt. Impulsive spending, a lack of financial knowledge, and failing to monitor expenses may lead to a debt cycle that causes difficulty and worry for individuals.

Uncertain financial priorities: Without a budget, it may be difficult for you to set priorities for your finances. This is because a budget provides a clear framework for allocating funds to specific goals, such as college preparation, house ownership, or retirement savings.

Ineffective Resource Allocation: Ineffective resource utilization is often the result of inadequate or nonexistent budgeting. You can find yourself overspending on unnecessary items or services if you don't monitor your spending and analyze your spending patterns. This would make it more difficult for you to conserve money and make wise investments.

Importance of Personal Budgeting

Financial Awareness: It's important to know your financial situation, and creating a personal budget helps you do so. It helps you track your expenditure, identify areas of unnecessary spending, and pinpoint areas where you may cut down on expenses or increase savings. Knowing this is crucial to building a solid financial foundation.

Goal Setting: By creating a personal budget, you may identify and work toward achievable financial goals. You can manage resources effectively and track your progress toward your objectives by using a budget. It ensures that the money you have worked so hard to earn is being used in a way that advances your objectives.

Flexibility and Adaptability: You understand that unforeseen costs and occurrences are a part of life. Because it provides a buffer for unanticipated costs and emergencies, establishing a personal budget acts as a safety net for your money. It helps you to adapt to changing circumstances and maintain financial stability even in difficult times.

Hints For Making a Personal Spending Plan

Making a personal budget is a crucial first step in obtaining financial independence and stability. Having the ability to purposefully manage your funds via budgeting fosters confidence and financial discipline. Consider using these steps to create a productive personal budget:

Monitor income and spending: To begin, thoroughly assess your sources of income and classify all of your out-of-pocket expenses. Utilize tools that may assist you in efficiently monitoring transactions, such as spreadsheets and other budgeting applications. This phase is essential for determining your spending habits and identifying potential areas for improvement. Sort your costs into categories for mandatory and optional spending, then prioritize them. Prioritize paying for your necessities first, including rent, electricity, and food. A portion of your salary should be placed away for savings in order to improve your financial stability and pay off any outstanding obligations.

Establish an Emergency Fund: Save a portion of your salary to cover unforeseen costs. By protecting you from unanticipated expenses and income disruptions, a safety net will provide financial security during difficult times.

Establish Realistic Goals: You should be sure to set long- and short-term financial goals that correspond with your objectives. Whether your objectives are to pay off debt, save for a trip, or build an emergency fund, setting realistic goals can help keep you motivated and give your budget a purpose. You may make a successful personal budget by using these easy pointers, but you should be aware that personal budgeting is a continuous process. Make sure you periodically evaluate and adjust your budget to account for changing needs, fluctuating income, and new financial goals. Be flexible and ready to make the necessary adjustments in order to maintain your budget in line with your evolving needs and goals.

You are able to take control of your financial destiny by creating your own personal budget. By being more aware of your income and spending, establishing realistic objectives, and regularly checking your budget, you may make informed financial choices and move closer to your desired financial outcomes.

Remember that the first step in managing your money is taking charge of them. With every step you take toward budgeting, you'll be one step closer to leading an independent and financially stable life. As a result, embrace the power of budgeting and let it motivate you to make prudent and confident financial choices. Think of yourself as someone who can secure a better financial future, and see how your dedication and self-control transform your life.

By adopting the discipline of budgeting, you may attain financial stability, reduce stress, and pave the way for a better and more prosperous future. Give yourself the ability to shape a great future by starting now.

B. Building an Emergency Fund: Protecting Yourself Against Financial Setbacks

A cash reserve put up expressly for unforeseen costs or financial problems is known as an emergency fund. Medical expenses, house repairs, auto repairs, and income loss are a few typical examples. Generally speaking, you may utilize emergency savings for any size unexpected expenditure or payment that isn't included in your regular monthly spending and expenses.

Why is it necessary for me?
If you don't have savings, even a little financial setback might cause you problems down the road, and if it results in debt, that damage could not go away. According to research, those who have a hard time getting over a financial setback tend to have less reserves to assist them in the event of another disaster. They

could depend on loans or credit cards, which might result in debt that is often more difficult to repay. To meet these expenses, they could also take money out of other investments, such as retirement accounts.

How much of it do I need?
Depending on your circumstances, you may need to establish a larger emergency savings account. Consider the most frequent kind of unforeseen expenditures you have experienced in the past, together with their associated costs. This might assist you in determining your desired amount to put away. Setting money away might be challenging if you don't get paid the same amount every week or month or if you live paycheck to paycheck. However, even a little sum may provide some monetary stability.

How should I construct it?
There are several approaches to begin saving money. These tactics address a variety of circumstances, such as having little capacity to save or having inconsistent income. You may be able to employ all of these tactics, but the simplest methods to get started are to manage your cash flow or set aside some of your tax return if you don't have much to save.

Method 1
Make saving a habit

Being able to save regularly makes it simpler to accumulate funds of any amount. It is one of the quickest methods to grow your savings. If you don't already save on a regular basis, here are some essential guidelines for developing and maintaining a savings habit:

Decide on an objective. Setting a clear objective for your savings will keep you motivated.

Establish a method for consistently contributing. There are many methods to save money, and one of the simplest is often to set up regular repeating payments, as you'll see below. Another option is to set away a certain amount of money every day, week, or pay period. Set a goal for a certain amount, and your savings will increase much more quickly if you can sometimes afford to do more.

Keep a close eye on your development. Establish a routine for checking your funds. Finding a mechanism to track your progress may provide satisfaction and motivation to keep going, whether it's by writing down a running tally of your contributions or receiving an automated alert about your account balance.

Honor your accomplishments. If you're continuing with your savings habit, use this chance to celebrate your accomplishments. Choose a few self-care techniques, and after you've accomplished your first objective, decide on your next one.

Method 2
Control your money flow

The time that your money comes in (from your revenue) and leaves (from your costs and spending) is what makes up your cash flow. Inaccurate timing may result in you running out of money at the end of the week or month, but if you monitor it often, you'll start to realize where you can make adjustments to your saves and expenditures. You might be able to negotiate with your creditors (landlords, utility providers, credit card companies, etc.) to change the dates on which your payments are due, or you could utilize the weeks when you have more money to transfer a little amount into savings.

Method 3
Utilize one-time chances to save money.

Additionally, there can be periods of the year when you get a large windfall. A tax refund is often one of the biggest cheques that people in the United States get each year. You could get a monetary present at other times of the year, such as on a birthday or holiday. Even though it would be easy to spend it all, keeping some or all of the money might enable you to swiftly accumulate emergency funds.

Method 4
Set up automatic savings
One of the simplest methods to start saving consistently and see your funds grow over time is to set up an automated savings account. Setting up recurring transfers via your bank or credit union to transfer money automatically from your checking account to your savings account is a popular method to do this. You will be consistently contributing to your savings after you have it set up, but you get to choose how much and how frequently.

But, it's a good idea to keep an eye on your balances to avoid paying overdraft penalties in the event that your checking account is depleted of funds at the time of the automated transaction. Consider adding calendar reminders or automated alerts to remind you to check your balance to help you remain attentive.

Method 5
Put money aside via labor

You may also set up automatic savings via your job. Apart from the employer-based retirement payments, you may be able to divide your salary between your savings and checking accounts. Ask your company whether splitting your paycheck across two accounts is feasible if you get it via direct deposit. This is a simple approach to save money aside without giving it much thought if you're tempted to spend your salary right away.

How much to save

Three to six months' worth of costs should be covered by an emergency fund, but accumulating that much money takes time. To get you started, set modest objectives like setting aside $5 per day. Next, gradually increase it to a reserve that can pay for many months' worth of expenditures.

Your income and spending will determine how much money you ultimately want to save. Prioritize meeting your needs rather than trying to make up for lost revenue. Typical essential monthly costs include housing, utilities, food, transportation, and loan or credit card payments.

Add up all of your monthly expenditures and multiply that amount by the number of months you would want to have extra cash for spending to figure how much you need to save. Aim for nine to twelve months' worth of spending in an emergency fund for single parents, company owners, or those with variable earnings, taking into consideration the increased unpredictability of their income.

Start your emergency fund in 7 simple steps.

1. Create a budget and identify areas where you can increase your savings.

A tried-and-true technique for managing your money and reducing expenditure is budgeting. Understanding where and how you spend is the first step in finding methods to save. Making a budget enables you to monitor or cut down on your spending and allocate your money more wisely. Budgeting App is one helpful tool that may assist you in calculating income and spending and giving you a dashboard picture of your financial status.

2. Establish your emergency fund target.

According to a 2022 poll conducted by the U.S. Bureau of Labor Statistics (BLS), the typical family spends $3,828 per month on housing, transportation, and food essentials. Making sure your family has enough money saved for these kinds of expenses is essential to setting your emergency fund target. A budget is a spending plan that assists you in figuring out how much money you'll need for monthly necessities. The amount you need to cover six months' worth of expenditures may be computed by adding up the monthly costs of housing, food, transportation, and other essentials, then multiplying the total by six. Most families may need some time to accomplish the six-month objective.

3. Establish a direct deposit.
Approximately 95% of Americans who participated in a 2023 American Payroll Association study said they received their paychecks using direct deposit. You no longer need to physically deposit checks when you use direct deposit, which automatically transfers your paycheck and other monies into your bank or savings account. However, you don't have to deposit all of your money into one account. By setting up a split direct deposit, you may choose a portion of your income to go into your emergency fund and the remaining amount to your bank account, or the other way around. Moreover, there are applications for savings that may automatically move a portion of your income into a savings account. Not only can automating the process make saving easier,

but it will also help you stay on course to meet your savings objectives.

4. Increase your funds gradually.

In December 2023, the Bureau of Economic Analysis reported that the personal saving rate in the United States was 3.7%. The proportion of disposable income that is saved is known as the personal saving rate. Increasing the amount you contribute to your emergency fund by 1% or a set amount each time you hit your savings target is one method to gradually raise your savings rate. It may be easier to hide the lesser transfer into your checking account if you increase the amount in little increments.

5. Set aside unforeseen cash

A financial windfall is when you get a large sum of money out of the blue. A few years later, 70 percent of people who acquire such a windfall won't have any money left, according to the American Institute of Certified Public Accountants. Unless you already have a sizable emergency fund built, at least a portion of every windfall you get should be utilized to add to it. Unexpected funds might arrive in the form of lottery or contest winnings, tax refunds, bonuses, monetary gifts, inheritances, or other sources.

6. Once your target is reached, continue saving.
As of 2022, the BLS estimates that the average cost of living is $72,967 per year. The longer you can survive on emergency savings in the event of a sickness or job loss, the more money you'll have on hand. Not every emergency calls for a six-month buffer. If you are hospitalized for many months or lose your job for more than a year, you will be happy that you have more money set aside in your emergency fund.

7. Start saving now with a bank account bonus.
Incentives in the form of cash are often provided by banks to attract new clients who create checking or savings accounts. The extra money might be used to start a new emergency fund or contribute to an already-existing one. Banks are now rewarding customers who establish new checking or savings accounts or who recommend friends and family with incentives of up to $3,000.

Making sure you're receiving the highest return on your investment is another method to boost your bank account balance in addition to searching for a bank account bonus. Online banks often provide the greatest rates as they don't have the expense associated with running physical locations.

Maintaining an orderly savings account will help you stay on track to reach your financial objectives. For example, keep your emergency savings in a different account than your vacation fund. By doing this, you may be able to save your emergency funds for other uses. You may divide your money into several buckets with certain bank accounts.

Where to keep it

It depends on your circumstances where you place your emergency money. This money should be kept in a location where it is secure, easily accessible, and unlikely to be spent on non-emergencies. You may choose the option that best suits your needs from the following alternatives for where to place your emergency savings:

Bank or credit union account: It may make sense to have a specific account where you may retain and manage these monies if you have an account with one of these institutions, which are often seen to be among the safest locations to deposit your money.

Prepaid card: A prepaid card allows you to put funds into it. You may only spend the amount that is on your card, and it is not affiliated with any bank or credit union.

Cash: Keeping emergency cash on hand, either at home or with a reliable family member or friend, is an additional choice. Remember that money may be lost, stolen, or destroyed.

When to use it.

Decide for yourself what expenses are unexpected or in case of an emergency. Try to maintain consistency even if every unforeseen cost isn't an immediate crisis. You could need it to cover a medical expense that wasn't covered by insurance. You may be able to stay out of debt by keeping a reserve cash for unforeseen expenses rather than depending on loans or other credit options. But if you need it, don't be scared to use it. Simply put, if you deplete your emergency funds, attempt to replenish it. It will become easier if you practice saving over time.

C. Managing Debt: Techniques for Effective Debt Repayment

Using budgeting and financial planning, debt management is a strategy for getting your debt under control. Utilizing these techniques to assist you in reducing your existing debt and moving toward its elimination is the aim of a debt management strategy. To assist you with your plan, you may either design a debt management strategy on your own or enroll in credit counseling.

The easiest course of action is to set up your own strategy, but sometimes having assistance or accountability from an outside partner may be beneficial. Plans for managing debt deal with unsecured debts such as credit card and personal loan balances. Typically, debt management takes place in one of two ways:

1. Self-help or do-it-yourself debt management
The first choice is a do-it-yourself debt management program. In this edition, you set a spending limit for yourself that will enable you to settle your bills and keep your finances stable. Do-It-Yourself approaches to managing debt include the debt avalanche and snowball techniques.

Avalanche debt repayment technique
Regardless of the approach you use, you should first aim to pay the minimal amount owed on all of your bills. Your credit will suffer if not. Paying down the debt with the greatest interest rate is the main goal of the avalanche debt payback strategy. After paying off the "mother of debts," you apply the money you have been contributing

to the obligation with the second-highest interest rate, and so on. The interest you save with this strategy is one

of its main advantages. The drawback is that you can have trouble maintaining your motivation since it might take some time to pay off your initial loan.

The snowball debt repayment plan
When using the snowball approach, you begin with the lowest payment and work your way up depending on the debt. The snowball debt technique has the major benefit of allowing you to experience victories sooner. Paying off your first debt is a really pleasant sensation, and if you achieve it early in the game, you probably won't be able to stop the momentum. The possibility of paying more interest on your debts is a drawback.

Who this is ideal for: If you have trouble controlling your spending but are able to pay off debt each month by practicing more discipline, this strategy can be helpful to you.

Principal benefits: Your credit score may be safeguarded by paying on time each month and in whole. To stay motivated during the repayment process, you may also design a practical plan with milestones and a debt-payoff date.

Principal drawbacks: You won't receive advice from an expert who could have better ideas on how to pay off

debt more quickly. Moreover, creditors may not be amenable to discussions.

Financial management tools, payback calculators, and budget calculators may all be used to help you stay on track. If necessary, you might strive to reduce your interest rates or monthly payments to your creditors in order to assist you pay off your debt. You may choose to maintain or terminate an account after the debt is under control.

Debt management with a credit counselor
The second method of debt management is credit counseling. The National Foundation of Credit Counselors can help you locate a credit counselor in your community. Credit counselors may be found in the charity and for-profit sectors. Before enrolling in a credit counseling program, read reviews and be aware of any costs that may apply.

If required, a credit counselor may negotiate a debt management plan (DMP) with your creditors in addition to assisting you in creating a strategy to pay off your obligations. In order to help you pay off debt more quickly, it often lasts three to five years and contains concessions such as a lower interest rate, a smaller monthly payment, or fee exemptions. The creditor may

cancel your accounts after each obligation is settled in order to prevent accruing further debt, depending on your specific situation. The ideal audience for this is anybody looking for expert assistance in managing their money and credit score.

Principal benefits: In general, paying off debt via a DMP is less expensive than paying off creditors straight. If discussions are successful, you will get a predetermined monthly payment and a schedule for paying off your debt. There will be no further collecting calls. Furthermore, if you pay the sums for less than you owe, it won't have as big of an effect on your credit score.

Drawbacks: The worst drawback is that you may not be able to access your credit accounts while the DMP is in effect. Additionally, you'll give the counseling organization power over your debts. Usually, the agency receives a single monthly payment, which could also include a monthly charge, and distributes it to your creditors.

Debt Settlement Business

Financial Makeover

To assist in paying off your outstanding credit card debt, you may also choose to work with a debt relief business. These profit-driven organizations engage in negotiations with lenders and creditors in order to arrive at settlement agreements that are lower than the total amount owed.

You will open an account with the debt reduction firm and begin making monthly payments there. Many debt relief organizations may advise you to stop making payments to lenders and creditors in the meantime in order to expedite the bargaining process.

You will be provided with the settlement after it has been agreed. If you consent, the payment will be made using money from the account you have been making payments into. A settlement fee will also be deducted from the same account by the debt reduction firm.

Who this is best for: People who are drowning in credit card debt and who would rather avoid filing bankruptcy or who have attempted self-settlement without much success may find debt relief to be excellent.

Benefits; The biggest benefit is that you might spend less each month towards your debts. If settlement proposals are accepted, you could be able to pay off debt more quickly and retain more of your money in your pocket.

Principal drawbacks: In addition to the possibility of getting you into legal trouble if your creditors and

lenders reject settlement proposals, paying off your debts for less than the total amount owed would probably lower your credit score. Also, if the amount forgiven exceeds $600, you could be required to pay federal income tax.

Counsel
1. Concentrate on Just One Debt

Whichever repayment plan you choose, be sure to concentrate on paying off one loan at a time. You'll make more progress and find it simpler to keep track of and handle your bills. Moreover, you may pay down more of the principal since you are concentrating your efforts on one obligation rather than dividing them across many ones. You'll therefore save more on interest.

2. Reduce Costs

Look for areas where you may save costs while paying off debt. Reducing your living expenditures allows you to apply more funds to your debt.

Here are some tips for cutting costs:

• Determine your out-of-pocket costs.

Determine your costs if you don't already have a budget. This covers everything, including groceries, entertainment, petrol, insurance, rent, bills, and monthly subscriptions.

•Aim for the large payouts.

Housing, transportation, and groceries are your three main expenditure areas. You may increase your monthly savings if you can cut costs in any one of these three categories.

• Go for the simple victories.

Recurring expenditures are a good place to start when cutting costs. This covers monthly subscriptions, payments, and auto insurance. Speak with the business to inquire about any discounts or try to work out a better price. By setting up autopay or making an annual payment rather than a monthly one, you may be able to save money. Eliminating items you're not using is another approach to get quick victories. For example, terminate your gym membership if it has been a while since you last visited.

3. Press "Pause" to Stop Taking on More Debt

While you are paying off debt, try to freeze or shut your credit card accounts. It's imperative that you refrain from taking on new debt while you're paying off existing debt.

If not, you might experience a sense of reversal and find yourself back at the starting point.

Note: Your credit may suffer if you close a credit card. This is because closing a credit card has an impact on

your credit usage ratio, also known as your balance-to-limit ratio. The sum owed on all of your cards divided by the total amount of all of your cards' maximum limits is your credit usage ratio.

Your credit usage ratio is 30% if the combined spending limit on all of your cards is $30,000 and you have a $9,000 debt. It is preferable to have a lower credit usage ratio. Generally speaking, you want to keep it under thirty percent. Depending on the credit card limit and the total amount owed, closing a credit card may negatively impact your credit score. Many credit cards now come with a "freeze card" option that allows you to temporarily press the "pause" button on your card if you're not quite ready to pay off your debt on them.

4. Contemplate Methods to Increase Revenue

Check to see whether your present employment offers any room for advancement so you can make more money. Use your important employer status to negotiate a raise or bonus if you have contributed to the company's profitability, efficiency, or reduction of stress on your team.

Look for side gigs that may help you make extra cash in addition to your current employment. There are many other options to supplement your income, including pet sitting, ride-sharing, teaching, freelance writing, and more. Put whatever additional money you get toward paying down your debt. This includes monetary gifts and little windfalls that come your way, in addition to money from a side job, bonus, or increase.

5. Keep an eye on your credit
You may assess how your debt reduction efforts are improving your credit while you pay off your debt by keeping an eye on your credit report. Generally, your score increases as you reduce your balances and pay off loans.

You can monitor your credit and check your credit score for free with a few different free credit monitoring programs. You may check your credit score via a number of well-known credit card firms and money management applications. To ensure that your balances, payment history, and other information are appropriately recorded, you should also get a copy of your credit report. You may spread out the free reports you receive from each of the three credit agencies during the course of the year.

6. Make Debt Repayment Simple

Even if it takes a lot of work, there are methods to make debt repayment "easier," so to speak. In addition to

haggling over the overdue amount, the following strategies might assist you in making payments on schedule:

•Put autopay in place.
It will be simpler to pay off your debt if you have to take fewer steps in the process. Automatically pay off all of your debts. It will guarantee payments on schedule.

•Make more payments.
Aim to make an additional payment each month in addition to the monthly minimum. Aim for weekly payments if you're feeling very ambitious.

•Try to reschedule the due dates for the payments.
Speak with your lenders to see if you may reschedule payments if you're experiencing trouble making your payments on time.

7. Recognize that it's an emotional trip

Having debt is associated with a lot of intense feelings. Grief, denial, humiliation, dread, tension, worry, and fury are a few examples. On some days, you could feel as if your debt is overshadowing your pleasure and delight. You know what? That is entirely typical.

It's good to know that you're not the only one who struggles with debt. By understanding that it's a process, and accepting the emotions that come with debt, you'll be able to manage your payments, and also have a good grip on your emotional and mental well-being.

Chapter Four

Implementing Smart Money Management Techniques

A. Saving and Investing: Growing Your Wealth Over Time

Even if money doesn't grow on trees, it can increase with prudent saving and investing. One of the most vital skills you'll ever need is knowing how to safeguard your financial security. You don't have to be an expert to be able to do that. All you have to do is establish a strategy, be prepared to follow it, and know a few fundamental things. Regardless of your financial situation, it's critical to inform yourself about your options. Nobody can promise that the investments you make will provide a profit. However, you should be able to achieve financial stability over time and reap the rewards of money management if you learn the truth about investing and saving and carry out a wise strategy.

To secure financial stability and a promising future, it is important to comprehend the distinction between investing and saving. Even though these words are sometimes used synonymously, it's crucial to understand that they are not the same. Starting early is a fantastic approach to position oneself for long-term financial security. Savings and investing are both essential components of personal finance.

How Does One Save?

Individuals save aside money for emergencies as well as for shopping. Setting money away for future needs is called saving, and it is a crucial component of personal finance. Consider it like investing in a piggy bank, only you may use a savings account or a certificate of deposit (CD) that accrues interest over time instead of a real piggy bank. One may save money for several purposes, such as purchasing a new device, planning a trip, or setting aside money for unforeseen costs in an emergency fund.

Saving money is a great method to reach short-term financial objectives and be ready for unforeseen events like auto repairs or medical expenses. Regular savings can help you build a cushion that will support you during difficult times. Although the return rates on savings are often modest, your money is still secure since they are low-risk investments.

An illustration

Putting some of your allowance or salary into a savings account each month is one way to save. For example, let's imagine you have ten months to save up $1,000 for a new laptop. You may achieve your goal without having to pay interest on a credit card or loan by saving away $100 a month. To guarantee that you continuously save without needing to remember to do it manually, you may also utilize automated transfers.

Benefits and Drawbacks of Saving

Savings provides many advantages, including being protected from loss, having cash on hand for purchases and other short-term objectives, and acting as a safety net against unforeseen expenses. There are, however, some disadvantages to take into account, such as losing out on potentially larger profits from riskier investments. Rising inflationary situations may also lead savings to lose buying power.

While saving is an important component of any financial plan, a balanced approach to financial planning requires combining saving with other types of investment, such as stock market investing or retirement savings.

What Does Investing Entail?

By putting your money to work in financial instruments like stocks, bonds, and mutual funds, investing allows you to see your money increase over time. Investing, as opposed to saving, entails some risk but also offers the possibility of longer-term, larger returns.

Investing will help you attain long-term financial objectives like retirement, a down payment on a home, or education savings. Selecting assets that fit your objectives, risk tolerance, and time horizon is crucial because investing entails taking on some risk. Since you will have more time to weather the ups and downs of the stock market, you can generally take on more risk the longer you can invest.

Let's take an example where you would want to invest in Apple. Purchasing stock in the firm entitles you to a small ownership stake in the development and profitability of the business. The stock in Apple may appreciate in value over time if the company does well, enabling you to sell it for a profit.

It's crucial to keep in mind that investing has no promises and that there's always a chance of losing money. For instance, your investment may be all but useless if Apple were to file for bankruptcy. To lower your risk, it is crucial to diversify your portfolio by making investments in a range of businesses and sectors.

An illustration

An excellent example of investing is using a 401(k) retirement plan, which requires you to put away a percentage of your salary to purchase stocks, bonds, and other financial instruments in a diverse portfolio with the aim of increasing your savings over time. A portion of your pay is what you put into the plan, and up to a certain level, your company could match your contribution. The plan administrator selects a portfolio of stocks, bonds, and mutual funds to be invested using the money you pay to the plan.

The primary benefit of using a 401(k) retirement plan is the tax advantages it provides. You pay less in taxes because the amount you give is subtracted from your taxable income. Furthermore, the growth of your 401(k) assets is tax-deferred, allowing your money to accumulate tax-free over time and perhaps provide better returns than a regular savings account. Taxes do not become payable until you begin taking withdrawals from the account.

Putting money into a 401(k) plan emphasizes how crucial it is to begin retirement savings as soon as feasible. You may take advantage of compound interest and perhaps increase your retirement savings by making regular investments over time. It's crucial to choose a mix of assets that complements your retirement objectives and risk tolerance. You should also periodically examine and tweak your investments over time to make sure they still match your requirements.

Benefits and Drawbacks of Investing

Investing may help you reach long-term financial objectives, like saving for retirement or purchasing a home, and it can potentially provide larger returns than savings accounts. Additionally, via compounding and reinvestment, investing can increase your wealth over time.

There are a few drawbacks, however, that must be taken into account. There is always some risk associated with investing, and there is no assurance that you will profit or even get your money back. Having a diverse portfolio of assets might be beneficial. It's essential to do due diligence and comprehend the possible hazards connected to various investment kinds. It might be challenging for some individuals to retain discipline and a long-term perspective while investing because of market volatility or the desire to follow the herd in an effort to earn immediate gains.

Knowing When to Invest and Save

Whether to invest or save money is one of the most frequent issues individuals have. Your unique financial status, as well as your objectives and risk tolerance, will determine the answer to this question.

Even if your income and costs may be restricted while you're young, it's never too early to begin saving and investing. In fact, getting a head start might provide you a big edge when it comes to gradually accumulating money. You may achieve long-term objectives by investing, such as retirement or education savings. You may invest in riskier items and take more chances since you have more time as a young person.

Long-term investment offers greater flexibility in terms of recovery and benefits, even in the event of short-term losses. Put another way, you may benefit from the force of compounding, which allows your money to increase enormously over time, by investing early and consistently.

Experts advise switching from riskier investments like equities to more conservative ones like bonds and cash as you age and have a shorter time horizon. This is due to the fact that if the market falls just before you want to retire, short-term volatility might pose a greater danger.

Saving money is usually a smart idea, even for younger people, especially if you have short-term objectives like paying for a trip, a new laptop, or a phone. Savings is the process of transferring funds into a low-risk, secure account, such as a certificate of deposit (CD), savings account, or money market account. Although savings products typically have little risk, they also often give poor returns. If you can't afford to lose any of your money and you need to access it soon, they're a fantastic choice.

Make sure you have enough money saved in an emergency fund to cover several months' worth of costs and enough in your savings account to meet all of your immediate necessities, such as rent, bills, and food, before you invest any money.

Why do some individuals choose saving money above making investments?

For a number of reasons, some individuals may choose to conserve money than make investments. More cash saved in an account for unforeseen costs or emergencies is preferred by some individuals as a feeling of security.

Others may choose to put the money in a low-risk savings account because they have more short-term financial objectives, such as saving for a down payment on a home or a trip. Furthermore, some individuals may not be knowledgeable or skilled enough to invest, or they might not have a high enough risk tolerance to feel comfortable taking on the degree of risk involved in investing. Lastly, after paying for their necessities, some individuals may not have any money left over for investments.

How much money should be invested as opposed to saved?

A person's unique financial objectives, risk tolerance, and unique situation all influence how much money should be saved vs invested. As a general guideline, you should have three to six months' worth of living costs saved up in an emergency fund. You should also have enough money in a savings account to pay for immediate expenditures like bills, and you should invest the remainder. Therefore, the precise amount that should be saved vs invested will vary based on criteria including age, income, debt load, and long-term financial objectives.

Getting Money to Invest or Save

Finding methods to reduce your costs is necessary if you are spending all of your income and never have any left over for savings or investments. You'll be shocked to see how little recurring costs that you can live without accumulate over the course of a year if you keep an eye on where your money is going. Purchasing a cup of coffee every day for only $1.00, which is a pretty reasonable price for a nice cup of coffee these days, comes to a total of $365.00 a year. If you were to save that $365.00 for a year and then invest it in something that yields 5% annually, your money would increase to

Financial Makeover

$465.84 after five years and $1,577.50 after thirty. That is "compounding"'s power.

You may earn interest on both the money you save and the interest it generates when you use compound interest. Even a little sum saved over time might grow to be a significant sum of money. You can increase money if you're prepared to keep an eye on your expenses and often hunt for little methods to save. It was accomplished with only one cup of coffee.

If a simple cup of coffee can have such a significant impact, consider how you may increase your income by cutting down on other expenses and saving that additional cash. If you are an impulsive buyer, set a rule that you will never purchase anything until 24 hours have passed. After a day, you may not want to purchase it. At the end of each day, try taking all the spare change out of your wallet and pockets. The rate at which those pennies and dimes pile up will amaze you!

Cash Out on a Credit Card or Other Debt with High Interest

When it comes to total returns, there aren't many investing plans that outperform or carry less risk than paying off all of your high-interest debt. Many carry credit cards in their wallets, some of which they have "maxed out"—that is, used to the full amount authorized.

When you don't have the money in your pocket or the bank, using a credit card might make it appear simple to make pricey purchases. Credit cards, however, are not free money.

The majority of credit cards have exorbitant interest rates—up to 18% or higher—if the amount isn't paid off in full each month. The best course of action if you have credit card debt is to pay off the amount owed in full as soon as you can. Almost no investment will provide the significant returns required to stay up with an interest rate of 18%.

It is thus preferable to pay off any credit card debt before putting money into savings. After paying off your credit cards, you may start saving and investing by creating a budget. Here are a few pointers for staying out of credit card debt:

Remove the Plastic
If your debt is reasonable and you are certain you will have the funds to pay the payment when it comes, don't use a credit card.

Recognize Your Debts
It's simple to lose track of the amount you've charged on your credit card. Calculate the amount you will owe each month and record the amount you spend each time you

use a credit card. If you are aware that you will not be able to pay the whole amount due, attempt to calculate how much you can afford to pay each month and how long it will take to pay the entire amount.

Debit the card with the highest interest rate.
If you owe money on many credit cards, pay off the one with the highest interest rate first. While you continue to just pay the minimum on your other cards, make as many monthly payments as you can toward that debt until it is completely paid off. The same guidance applies to any other high-interest loan that does not have the same tax benefits as, say, a mortgage (8% or more).
What options do you have now that you have paid off your credit cards and started putting money away for savings and investments?

Increasing Revenue
To put it simply, there are two methods to get money.
1. You labor for pay.
You either own your own firm or are paid by someone else to work for them.

2. You benefit from your money.
You take that money and either invest or save it.

How to Put Your Money to Work

Your funds generate income. Your money could produce a consistent salary if it is put to use. For a certain amount of time, someone pays you to spend their money. You get your money back along with "interest." Alternatively, if you purchase stock in a business that regularly distributes "dividends" to its shareholders, the business could give you a percentage of its profits. Like you, your money can generate an "income." When you work for your money, you might earn more of it.

You spend your money on something that could appreciate in value. You acquire ownership of something you think will appreciate in value over time. You sell it in the hopes that someone else would pay you more when you need your money back. For example, you purchase a plot of land with the expectation that its value would rise as more companies or residents come into your community. You figure that in five, ten, or twenty years, you'll sell the land and someone else will purchase it for a lot more than you spent. Your money may sometimes be able to accomplish both simultaneously—earn a consistent income and appreciate in value.

Which investments make the most sense for me?
The answer will vary depending on your objectives, when you need the money, and if you can afford to lose your capital on a risky investment.

For example, if you are saving for retirement and you have 35 years to go before you retire, you might want to think about investing in riskier products. This is because you know that if you stick to only "savings" products or less risky products, your money will grow too slowly, or you might lose the purchasing power of your money due to taxes and inflation. Investing money that one will not need for a very long time in low-interest assets is a common error individuals make.

However, you should avoid making hazardous investment choices if you are saving for a short-term goal—five years or less—because you could have to incur a loss when it comes time to sell. Given that assets often experience dramatic price fluctuations, you should be certain that you have the patience to wait for the ideal moment to sell.

What is the purpose of investments?

Giving money to a business or venture in the hopes that it will succeed and repay you with even more money is what it means to make an investment.

Bonds and Stocks

Purchasing stocks or bonds is an option that many firms provide to their investors. This example demonstrates the differences between stocks and bonds. Let's imagine you think investing in a car manufacturer could be a smart idea. Everyone you know is purchasing one of its vehicles, and according to your acquaintances, the company's vehicles seldom break down and continue to function effectively for years.

You may either conduct the research yourself or have an investing specialist look into the firm and read as much as they can about it. You're certain after doing your homework that this is a reliable firm that will sell a lot more automobiles in the coming years.

The automaker sells bonds in addition to stocks. The corporation promises to repay your original investment in 10 years along with 8% annual interest payments twice a year on the bonds.Purchasing stock entails accepting the risk that, should the firm perform badly or the stock market decline in value, you might lose all or part of your original investment.

However, it's also possible that the stock will appreciate more than the bonds would. You will get your money back plus an annual interest rate of 8% if you purchase the bonds. And since the firm has been there for a long time and doesn't seem to be in danger of going bankrupt, you believe it will be able to keep its word to you about the bonds. The firm has a long history of producing automobiles, and as you are aware, its stock has increased in value by 9% year on average. In addition, the company has always distributed a 3% dividend from its earnings to its owners.

Why do some investors not succeed?
There are a number of reasons why individuals can find investing difficult. A typical cause is inexperience or ignorance, which may result in bad financial choices. Emotional biases like fear or greed may also lead to hasty or illogical judgments made by investors that might cost them money. It takes patience, discipline, and a long-term view to invest well, yet it may be challenging to stick with a plan when the market is volatile.

Why some investments provide profits while others don't.
•An investment may yield profits if the firm outperforms its rivals.
• The firm earns profits, meaning they make enough money to pay you dividends on your stock or interest on your bond when the time comes to sell your investment because other investors know it's a strong company.

You may lose money in the following situations:
• The company's rivals outperform it.
• The items or services offered by the organization are not desired by customers.

- The firm's executives do a poor job of running the company; they overspend and have more costs than revenues.

- Some investors, who you would have to sell to, believe that the stock price of the firm is excessively high considering its track record and prospects.
- The company's executives are deceitful. Rather than spending your money for the company, they spend it on holidays, clothing, and residences.
- They fabricate financial figures to mislead investors, or they lie about any part of the company, such as previous or future earnings that are not there or contracts they don't have to sell their items.
- The stock brokers influence the price of the company's shares to make it seem lower than its actual worth. These brokers dump the stock after driving up the price, which causes the price to drop and causes investors to lose money.
- When the market is down, you must sell your investment for any reason.

The Final Word
Both investing and saving are crucial elements of a sound financial strategy. While investing offers the possibility of larger long-term returns and may assist in achieving long-term financial goals, saving offers a safety net and a means of achieving short-term

objectives. It's important to note that losing money is a possibility while investing. Every strategy has advantages and disadvantages, so it's critical to strike the

best balance for your objectives and financial status. In the end, a comprehensive strategy that incorporates both investing and saving may help increase wealth, guard against financial shocks, and provide the groundwork for a more secure financial future.

B. Increasing Your Revenue: Investigating Different Revenue Sources

Investigating and cultivating several revenue sources is often necessary to achieve financial stability and increase your wealth. You may boost your earning potential and build a stronger financial foundation by diversifying your sources of income. We'll go over a number of tactics in this post to assist you in seeing and seizing chances to increase your income.

Make Use of Your Knowledge and Experience:
Your knowledge and experience may be a great resource for earning extra money. Think about providing people or companies in your field with freelancing or consulting services. With a little expertise and experience, you may start a side business that can help you advance your

career while simultaneously increasing your income. Determine your special talents and abilities to begin, then look into possible customers or markets for your services. Create a compelling value proposition and use professional channels, social media, and networking to promote your services.

Invest in Passive Income Opportunities:
Passive income is an attractive way to increase your income since it requires little to no continuous work on your side. Peer-to-peer lending, rental properties, dividend-paying investments, and royalties from creative works are examples of common passive income streams.

Determine your financial objectives, risk tolerance, and the amount of time and money you're prepared to commit to researching and evaluating prospective passive income alternatives. Remember that although certain passive income sources may need a one-time or capital expenditure, they could be well worth the effort in the long run due to the potential rewards.

Follow Your Entrepreneurial Dreams:
A fulfilling method to boost your income and reach financial independence is to launch a small company or follow your entrepreneurial dreams. Through entrepreneurship, you may explore your creativity,

enthusiasm, and aspirations while developing a possible avenue for rapid revenue development.

Make sure you thoroughly evaluate your ideas, resources, and market potential before starting your own business. Create a thorough company strategy and think about consulting mentors or business development experts to assist you deal with the difficulties and complications of becoming an entrepreneur. Investing in your professional development can pay off handsomely in the form of higher earning potential.

Upskill and Advance Your Career:
You can put yourself in a position to be promoted, have your pay increased, and have higher-paying job opportunities by upskilling and looking for career advancement opportunities. To broaden your skill set and stay up to date in your field, think about getting more certifications, going to workshops, or signing up for pertinent classes. Your career can also advance and new opportunities can arise if you network and establish relationships with leaders, mentors, and peers in the industry.

Finding and seizing different income-generating opportunities requires a proactive and strategic approach if you want to maximize your earnings. Your full earning potential can be unlocked and a stronger financial foundation can be built by utilizing your skills and expertise, investing in passive income sources, pursuing

entrepreneurial endeavors, and advancing your career. Having a variety of sources of income can help you reach your long-term financial objectives and feel more secure financially while also giving you the flexibility and freedom to follow your passions.

C. Making Well-Informed Financial Decisions: Steering Clear of Common Money Errors

People who want to secure their financial future and reach their financial objectives must make well-informed financial decisions. Being knowledgeable about finances can assist people in making decisions that are in line with their financial goals, whether they are managing their spending, investing, or saving for retirement.

Nine crucial pointers to assist you in making wise financial decisions are covered in this book. You can take charge of your finances and make long-term decisions that will benefit you by paying attention to these pointers.

1. Get Knowledge

You must educate yourself about various financial products, tools, savings, and personal finances in order to make wise financial decisions. Educate yourself with

books, seminars, credible financial websites, and financial news updates.

Learn about the various kinds of debts that exist, such as payday loans, credit cards, credit lines, and short-term loans. You will be able to make wise decisions if you comprehend ideas like compound interest, risk management, and investing strategies.

2. Establish Specific Financial Objectives

It's crucial to have certain objectives in mind before making any financial choices. Establish your financial goals, such as saving for a down payment on a home, an emergency fund, or college. Establishing SMART (specific, measurable, attainable, relevant, and time-bound) objectives will provide you a clear financial decision-making process.

3. Establish a spending plan

One of the most important steps in making wise financial choices is budget creation. To begin understanding your spending habits, start by keeping track of your income and expenditures. Sort the things in your expenditures by necessity and non-necessity. Set aside a certain percentage of your salary for investments and savings. You may prioritize your spending and make sure you are living within your means by creating a well-planned budget.

4. Evaluate Your Capacity for Risk

It's important to know how much risk you can afford to take when choosing investments. Certain people are willing to take on greater risks in exchange for perhaps larger rewards, whereas others would rather take more cautious measures. Determine your risk tolerance by taking into account your time horizon, financial objectives, and degree of comfort. This will assist you in selecting investments that suit your level of risk tolerance.

5. Make Diverse Investment

One of the most important concepts in making wise financial choices is diversification. Investing in a variety of asset types, such as bonds, real estate, and stocks, may help lower risk. You may be able to lessen the effects of market swings and shield your portfolio from big losses by diversifying.

6. Consult a Professional

Getting expert guidance might be helpful when making complicated financial choices. Financial advisers may provide professional advice suited to your individual objectives and requirements. They can guide you

through retirement planning, tax planning, investment possibilities, and other financial issues. To make sure you get trustworthy advice, choose a respected adviser who is subject to Financial Conduct Authority (FCA) regulation.

7. Examine and Modify Frequently

Financial choices shouldn't be predetermined. Review your financial status on a regular basis and make any necessary adjustments to your plan. Your financial choices may need to be adjusted over time in response to changes in your personal objectives, the state of the market, and your life circumstances. Remain proactive and make adjustments to guarantee that your choices continue to meet your changing demands.

8. Refrain from Making Rash Decisions

Impetuous financial choices might have repercussions down the road. Refrain from acting rashly due to feelings or fads in the market. Before making any big financial choices, take your time and do some research, analysis, and evaluation of your possibilities. Think about the advantages and disadvantages, and get assistance if necessary.

9. Learn from Errors

It's possible that financial choices don't always work out as planned. It's important to develop from your errors and see them as teaching moments. Think back on previous choices, pinpoint areas that need work, and modify your strategy appropriately. You may improve your future financial decision-making by using the lessons you've learned from your blunders.

It is possible to improve one's ability to make wise financial judgments with preparation, dedication, and understanding. You can make wise financial decisions that will serve you well in the long run by establishing clear goals, making a budget, learning about the market, evaluating your risk tolerance, diversifying your investments, consulting a financial advisor, reviewing and adjusting your finances on a regular basis, avoiding rash decisions, and taking lessons from your mistakes. Recall that financial choices affect your future greatly, so you should approach them thoughtfully and carefully.

Common Financial Mistakes To Avoid

Saving money has become more important to us as a result of the recent spike in expenses for everything from groceries to electricity. Though there are plenty of money-saving advice available, have you ever thought about the blunders to avoid?

The most frequent financial blunders that might cost you money are about to be revealed.

1. Excessive expenditure

Even while treating yourself is a wonderful idea, one of the worst financial blunders is overspending. Whether you purchase lunch every day or go out to eat often, these expenses may quickly mount up. For instance, if you spend $6.50 per week on a coffee and lunch combo, you would spend $338 in a year. You might increase the amount you have saved for a rainy day by routinely analyzing your expenses or finding places where you could make saves.

2. You don't ever go over your budget.

Though it might be intimidating at first, thinking and acting on your money can eventually pay dividends. There are other methods to cut costs, such as haggling over broadband price increases or comparison shopping for the best offers. You may also be able to prevent losing money on services you no longer use, such as a gym membership, by reviewing your direct debits every few months.

3. Neither a budget nor an emergency fund exist for you.

Your finances may be completely changed by creating a budget, which enables you to identify your spending patterns and make required reductions. A budget may assist you in determining how much you can save and how long it will take you to achieve any long-term objectives, like purchasing your first house. An emergency fund may also assist you deal with any unpleasant shocks since life can be unexpected.

Establishing an emergency fund equivalent to three to six months' worth of your monthly expenses is a smart move if you don't already have one. In this manner, you will be able to deal with unexpected large bills or job loss without having to take out costly loans.

4. Discovering unanticipated costs

Charges that are not immediately apparent, such as penalties for overdraft fees or late credit card payments, may add up. It's a good idea to remember when contracts are about to expire and when payments are due. For instance, during the expiration of your mortgage, you will be transferred to the Standard Variable Rate (SVR), which is often more costly.

5. Not setting aside enough money for retirement

Even though it's simple to put off retirement savings, you'll save more the sooner you begin. A little investment may grow into a larger savings account because of pensions' tax benefits and compound interest, which allows you to earn interest on your interest. Your company will pay to your workplace pension if you have one; if you raise your contributions, some employers may match the minimal amounts.

6. Making credit card purchases at ATMs
Do you own a credit card? Never use it to take money out of an ATM. Not only will you be charged a fee, but this will also appear on your credit report and might raise suspicions with prospective lenders. It's advisable to use a debit card to make withdrawals if you need cash.

7. Overtaxing or not receiving pension tax benefits
There are several ways to find yourself overpaying taxes. For instance, if you change employment or take money out of your pension and HMRC uses the incorrect code, you may be charged emergency tax. You must apply for further tax relief for the money you contribute to your pension if you are a higher-rate or additional-rate taxpayer. If you believe you have overpaid tax or are losing out on tax relief, it is preferable to contact HMRC.

8. Not obtaining coverage
Insurance is crucial, regardless of whether you want to travel or just want to protect your vehicle and possessions. To avoid being caught off guard by the tiny

print, it's a good idea to shop around and confirm that your insurance covers everything you need it to. Although the cost of insurance varies based on your situation, it's often less expensive than not having any protection in place in case anything unforeseen occurs.

9. Remaining a devoted client

Although it's simple to think that sticking with your bank or other service provider would benefit you, this isn't always the case. For instance, by moving to a different provider, you could be eligible for financial compensation, improved internet service, or a complimentary gift. Finding the greatest bargain for you always pays off, particularly if there will soon be a price increase.

10. Carelessly using credit cards

Getting a credit card tailored to your needs is a fantastic option if you need a 0% credit card.

For instance, you may stretch out the expense of a large purchase, lower the cost of your debt, or raise your credit score by using a 0% credit card. In addition, some purchases come with Section 75 protection. If your credit card has a 0% interest offer for a short period of time, you should make sure you pay off the minimum amount each month and have a strategy in place to pay off your debt since the interest rate may be quite high once it expires.

Financial Makeover

Chapter Five

Overcoming Financial Challenges

A. Dealing with Unexpected Expenses and Financial Emergencies

Regardless of how well you plan your spending and budget, unforeseen costs will always arise. You should be prepared for any unexpected expenses or medical emergencies and know what to do in them. You may use an emergency fund as a covert financial tool to handle unforeseen expenses. It serves as an insurance account that is solely utilized for these kinds of costs. In this manner, you may always have cash on hand for any kind of emergency. What are some strategies for handling unforeseen costs, then? You will be able to discover more about them with the help of this book.

1. Establish a definite plan
Preparing ahead of time is one of the greatest methods to handle unforeseen costs. You may stay out of financial danger and prevent overspending by making and adhering to a budget. Assessing your income and expenditure is the first move in this direction. Find out

how much you can afford to budget each month for unforeseen expenses. Next, jot out a list of all the possible costs that can arise, including house repairs, auto repairs, medical bills, and any other expenditures that you think might result in an emergency.

As soon as you have a clear understanding of what you are battling with, begin putting money away every month to build up a buffer. An emergency fund will help you stay out of debt by covering unforeseen costs. Breathe deeply and keep in mind that you have a strategy in place to handle unforeseen expenses. If you prepare a little, you can weather any financial storm.

2. Put Money Aside
One of the easiest strategies to save money is to have some cash on hand. Even if you may not be able to save for everything, having a little emergency fund can help you cover unforeseen expenses. Place funds into your savings account.

3. Get Ready
You ought to be prepared to handle unforeseen costs. Maintain an emergency reserve so that you can cover unforeseen costs. Verify that your insurance covers both medical expenses and auto repairs. This will assist you with avoiding financial difficulties in the event of an

unforeseen event. Spend less and save for bigger purchases so you have cash on hand if necessary.

4. Be Aware of Your Choices

These days, it's essential to be ready for everything since you never know what can occur. Many people's spending habits put them in difficult financial positions. It is thus essential to be aware of some of your alternatives in case of emergency.

5. Reducing Other Outlays

Individuals seldom consider their purchases before making them, and for most, reducing spending may seem like a very difficult choice. This will undoubtedly lead to the worst scenario ever later on. Reduce your spending as much as you can to provide a solid cushion for your budget. You may contribute a little more money in this manner to assist with the additional finances required.

6. Make Use of a Credit Card

If your credit history is strong, using a credit card might be a useful way to handle unforeseen bills. To avoid financial hardship from the lump sum payment, you may pay for your products in installments. It becomes simple to make payments and to ensure that you do it on time in order to consistently prevent accruing higher sums and having an impact on your credit score.

7. Remain composed

An unforeseen cost may quickly become a source of worry. The only way you can think clearly about what to do is to stay composed. How much does the loss cost? To what extent will there be expenses? When will you be able to get the money together to pay for it if you don't have it now?

Now that you know what's required, you need to start looking for answers. If you don't currently have the money, consider strategies to reduce other outlays or earn the additional money required to pay for the item.

8. Offload Certain Items

Selling certain assets is one way to handle unforeseen costs. Selling valuable items you no longer need might be a great strategy to acquire the funds you need to pay for your bills. Make sure you investigate an item's worth before selling it to ensure you get a reasonable price.

9. Take Initiative

There are a few proactive steps you may take to prepare for unforeseen costs. Keep an eye on your expenditures to determine how and why you are using your money. This will provide you with the data and figures you'll need to make any required reductions. Lastly, make an effort to plan ahead so that you can deal with unforeseen circumstances and be ready for anything.

10. Consider the Cost
There are many ways to assess an expenditure and determine if it is cost-effective.

•Consider how often you plan to utilize the item or service. Purchasing a product or service is an investment if you plan to use it daily.

•How much time will it last? It may not be worth the money if something has to be changed often.

•Think about the item's quality. The endurance of high-quality goods and services makes them well worth the investment of time.

11. Put a halt to your spending
Freezing your spending is one of the first things you can do when you have unforeseen bills to cope with. This entails cutting out on frivolous purchases and concentrating just on necessities. You may do this to help you save money for unforeseen costs.

Making a budget is one of the greatest techniques to stop spending. You may monitor your expenses in this manner and make sure that you only spend money on necessities. Establish a budget and start reducing your expenditures. For instance, cut down on eating out or purchase fewer branded items.

12. Create a Plan for Paying Off Debt

Planning ahead for difficult situations is usually a smart idea. You may then pay off all of your debt or spend all of your money. This savings account ought to be used exclusively. In this manner, the money will be there for you when you need it, and you won't have to charge the bill to your credit card. Whichever tactic you decide on, having a plan is essential. In this manner, you will keep your money intact in case of unforeseen needs and prevent taking on debt.

13. Make a plan for the future.

It's always necessary to plan ahead. In the event that you ever find yourself in need, having a well-thought-out financial plan will make it easier for you to pay off debt. Because you are already saving, you won't have to worry about bouncing a check or not having enough money for an unforeseen emergency. It's difficult for humans to plan for every possible aspect. However, you'll be more equipped to handle unforeseen costs if and when they arise if you give them some thought.

B. Handling Financial Setbacks: Strategies for Bouncing Back Stronger

Anyone may experience it. Everything is good one moment, and then something bad occurs, like a job loss, a sickness, or a terrible accident. Even if at the time it seems like nothing can help your bank account or heart, you can ultimately overcome financial losses like these. This book will guide you through the steps you may take to gradually improve both your emotional and financial well-being.

What kind of monetary obstacles should I budget for?

While no one likes to think about catastrophes, it's wise to be aware of the potential effects that certain disasters might have on your money. Different scenarios call for different considerations. In the event of the worst, there are additional factors to take into account and actions you may be able to take, depending on the circumstances. Here are a few instances of monetary losses.

•Loss of employment. Your income, insurance, and other benefits are dependent upon your employment. You could be eligible to keep your insurance or get severance money in certain circumstances, such as a layoff, but such benefits are often expensive and don't last forever.

•A significant asset loss. This might be your house, place of work, or automobile. Insurance may assist in recovering some of your losses in the event of an accident or tragedy, but replacing lost items or determining what to do next can be very expensive.

•Serious sickness. Even a good savings account might be depleted by medical expenditures, especially because there is no assurance on the duration of ailments and treatments. However, health and varied critical care, accidents, and disability can restrict some of these costs.

•Loss of a romantic lover. Divorce and death are two examples of losing a relationship. Breakups are another. You may be able to get benefits from your partner's life insurance, but you could also have to pay for the burial and any related obligations. Your housing expenses could go up after a separation, and while a divorce might result in some financial benefit, you might have to pay for legal counsel and adjust to living without cost-sharing.

A financial setback may also be made even more dramatic by a combination of low-level causes, such as

moving to a more costly area, changing one's spending habits, or rising expenses, or by the more subtle setbacks that build up over a number of years. Alternatively, you could see that you've been in a silent financial spiral after taking a look at your credit cards and bank account. Fortunately, it may be simpler to change those factors, so addressing them immediately will help you stop and turn around your situation.

Planning generally won't always equate to prevention in this situation. However, should you have a financial setback, having a healthy emergency savings fund or even a strategy for what you may sell or modify would help you react more skillfully.

The methods of recovering from a financial setback
It will take time to recover financially from any of the aforementioned. However, there are ways to approach recuperation more tolerably and increase your chances of regaining your balance by the attitudes and decisions you make.

•Recognize that you are not alone. Everyone will experience something similar at least once in their lifetime; your friends, neighbors, and relatives have all

Financial Makeover

experienced it. It is OK to be impacted by unpredictable, unanticipated events or to have made a few bad choices

that had disastrous consequences, but you have the power to choose your response, and that choice may have a significant influence on your ability to recover financially.

•Recognize your available alternatives. Strike a balance between analyzing your financial status and becoming angry. You may plan or determine what you can examine by taking a clear, in-depth look at what you have at your disposal. It could also give you a sense of productivity and encourage resilience and creativity.

•Focus your efforts on creating a budget. Examine the costs you need to prioritize and the things that you no longer need in the present. Knowing that these decisions will increase your chances of surviving the scenario will allow you to be harsh and prepare for significant spending cuts.

•Plan ahead. What condition will you want to be at the end of this phase? What happens if there is no improvement in your health? Can you withstand a sustained revenue decline over time? Answering these questions may be difficult and even unpleasant, but it can also be an opportunity to reconsider and rediscover your ideals. For example, maybe you've always desired to move to a stunning nation where the cost of living is reduced. Selling your home is a step toward that objective as well as helping you get back on your financial feet. Furthermore, planning forward enables you to see yourself in a different circumstance than the one you find yourself in, which may motivate you to come up with solutions and maintain them in the future.

•Request assistance. This goes beyond just requesting financial assistance. This involves organizing your bills and your approach to them with the assistance of qualified financial consultants or close, trustworthy friends and family. It might take the form of asking your loved ones for advice or a gut feeling while making decisions. It may even take the form of speaking with creditors and hospitals to arrange payment schedules. It might be difficult to consider help during a crisis, but there are many different kinds of it.

•Proceed at the necessary pace. In times of financial crisis, you may need to take immediate action to halt the bleeding. This may include selling assets to raise money, asking for a loan, or withdrawing a sizable portion of your emergency fund. It's important to know when time is of the importance since it may happen in certain scenarios. However, there are instances when taking too much time might close doors that could have opened up with a little more consideration and perseverance.

Though it may be inspiring, panic impairs judgment. More crucially, processing emotions is necessary in order to respond to financial losses. Losing a lover, for instance, might cause such a degree of emotional upheaval that you may not make decisions with your heart and mind more clearly.

Financial failures include more than simply monetary losses. They have the power to shake your whole worldview. However, you can overcome them and use the opportunity to really reevaluate your priorities in life.

C. Building Resilience: Cultivating a Positive Money Mindset

Money is a difficult subject. It is necessary for everyone to exist, but insufficient amounts may be very stressful. One may acquire a negative and damaging financial thinking process as a result of financial hardship or excessive debt. A person may not even be aware of how this style of thinking affects their money until it has been ingrained in them. You might jeopardize your chances of earning more money or paying off debt if you are always afraid of money. You need to change your perspective because if you ignore your money entirely, you'll just end up getting further into debt. Here are some pointers to get you started in developing a good money mentality.

•Pardon Your Previous Financial Errors

Nobody is flawless. It's likely that throughout the years, you have made a number of poor financial judgments. Maybe you went on too many shopping sprees or overpaid for rent because you fell in love with a gorgeous home, and now your credit cards are completely depleted. All of your previous choices have already happened. It's possible that past errors are still having an impact on you, but you don't have to constantly criticize yourself for them. Not everyone is taught how to handle money effectively since it might be difficult. Many individuals learn their lessons by making mistakes. The two most crucial things to concentrate on are self-forgiveness and learning from your errors.

When it comes to the bad choices you've made in the past, you should also attempt to reframe your thoughts. If you are in debt, reflect back on your social gatherings, travel experiences, and educational expenses. You made memories and had delight from your debt. Don't romanticize it, but keep in mind that it has a function. It's neither a hostile place or an abyss from which you can

never return. It was there for you when you needed it, and now you can work toward paying it off so you can go on with an even better life.

• Recognize your feelings and thoughts around money
Even while you may believe you know how you think about money, a closer examination may reveal some surprising information. Try this out: For a whole day, following every purchase or financial choice you make, sit down and write down your feelings. What's going through your mind right now? What is your emotional state? Be truthful and meticulous. When everything is said and done, review everything with an open mind. You may discover that certain areas of your money are causing you more worry than you anticipated, or you may discover that a purchase you had anticipated would make you happy really made you feel guilty after a little period of satisfaction. While it's perfectly OK to sometimes treat yourself, you should also consider the true impact of your spending patterns on your emotional, and mental well-being.

- **Acknowledge That It Is a Losing Game to Compare Yourself to Others**

One of the most risky things you can do in life is to compare yourself to other people; the same goes for money. To begin with, comparisons are seldom precise.

There is a warped lens. You are the most knowledgeable person about yourself, but if you compare yourself to a celebrity, an Instagram user, or a fictitious character, you are essentially comparing yourself to someone with whom you are unfamiliar. Facebook is a fake. People just let you see what they want you to.

They only share the best parts of their financial and personal journeys on social media. For example, you may come across an Instagram user who shares pictures of their gorgeous house, fashionable clothing, and lavish trips, but you have no idea how much debt they have on their credit cards. You have no idea whether they owe their parents thousands of dollars or are two months delinquent on their vehicle payment. They won't tell you about that portion of their life, so you'll never know. You can see why it is misleading and risky to compare your complete narrative with only a highlight reel of theirs, since you are continuously confronted with the darker side of your own.

You're in a comparable circumstance even if you're comparing yourself to friends or relatives. You can never really comprehend someone else's financial status or the considerations that go into difficult choices since you can never know as much about them as you do about yourself. Another drawback is that you risk being

frustrated if you compare yourself to others and discover that you are losing. Rather than concentrating on the good, you're concentrating on the bad. Your objectives begin to seem unachievable. You pay more attention to your shortcomings than to your progress. These kinds of thoughts have the potential to hinder you and ultimately lead to additional poor financial choices.

•Aim to Establish Positive Habits
Don't avoid talking about your money. Instead, make time each week to review your spending patterns, budget, and bills. Emphasize the areas that need development and give yourself a pat on the back for any accomplishments. Ignoring a problem won't make it go away. Instead, ignore your worries and take on the issues head-on.

Establish reasonable objectives for yourself and treat yourself modestly when you achieve them. Since neither your success nor your money got out of control overnight, it's critical to establish a number of little objectives and recognize each accomplishment.

•Make a Budget That Makes You Happy

A budget usually causes anxiety in individuals. Many see a budget as limiting and restrictive, yet this need not be the case. A flexible budget will help you recognize

your limits and keep within your spending limits while yet giving you permission to sometimes reward yourself. Generally speaking, you should allocate half of your monthly income to bills and requirements. You should set aside twenty percent of your salary for savings or debt repayment. Thirty percent is yours to do with as you like. It may be time to take a closer look at your monthly expenses and see which ones you can reduce or eliminate if you discover that you are unable to stick to this schedule.

• Recall to express gratitude

Embrace your current situation and express gratitude for whatever you have, even if it may not be as much as you would want. Give thanks for things like a roof over your head, a job that pays your bills, a vehicle that gets you about, food in your refrigerator, etc. Making more money and improving your life is something you can do at any stage in life, but it won't be sufficient until you learn to be thankful for what you already have. You and your ideas shouldn't be controlled by money. Rather, you should try to manage the way you think about money so that you can start to better regulate how much you spend. Start with these pointers, and see how your attitudes and ideas about money begin to positively impact your life.

Chapter Six

Maintaining Financial Wellness

A. Monitoring Your Progress: Tracking Your Financial Goals

Managing finances is difficult. A budget, spending priorities, prudent investing, financial goal-setting, and regular monitoring are all necessary. Although it may seem simple to create financial objectives, it is crucial to monitor them in order to determine the success of your financial plans and if any adjustments are required.

Everybody has different and distinct financial objectives. As such, it is impossible to standardize their measurement. Nonetheless, there are a few generic metrics that are conveniently used to monitor financial objectives periodically. When establishing these indicators, it's crucial to keep in mind that they ought to be simple to measure. You won't be able to attain your objectives just by establishing them. Maintaining timely records to evaluate advancements and deviances is equally crucial to long-term financial security.

The following four crucial indications will make it simple for you to monitor your financial objectives:

1. Net Worth
This is a really simple way to monitor the progress of your financial goals. For many years, calculating one's net worth has made managing finances easier for individuals. It has shown to be helpful in guiding individuals toward a better understanding of their financial situation by comparing their debt to their assets. They can clearly see their assets compared to their obligations, thanks to it.

Liabilities in this context include things like current outstanding loans, mortgages, credit card payments, rent, etc., whereas assets might include things like bank balances, real estate, cash deposits, investments and retirement accounts, houses, cars, and insurances. Your current financial status may be represented by your net worth, which is the result of deducting these liabilities from your assets. This amount should cover your financial objectives, such as retirement, vacation, home ownership, etc. The amount you extract should preferably be more than your targets as it will provide you more leeway to cover unforeseen, urgent costs.

Furthermore, in order to get a more equitable representation of the situation, it is crucial to contrast your net worth with non-investment, consumable assets like a home, vehicle, etc. A relative net worth (RNW) may be obtained by comparing net worth to consumable assets. This will show you how much of these assets are needed to maintain your present standard of living.

Net Worth / Consumable Assets equals RNW.

Therefore, your RNW should be sufficient (preferably over 100%) to support your present lifestyle and reach your desired financial goals in order to determine if you are on the correct route to reaching your financial objectives. It's also critical to remember that this indicator should be increased with time and computed semi-annually.

2. Credit Rating

A person's creditworthiness is measured by their credit score, to put it literally. It is a very potent gauge of one's financial well-being and progress toward financial objectives. If a person misses payments on their credit card, mortgage, loan premiums, or other obligations, their credit score will suffer. A poor credit score is a clear sign of bad finances and a sluggish rate of economic growth. A poor credit score might also

indicate unmet present demands and unfulfilled aspirations for the future. On the other hand, a good credit score suggests that you have enough money to cover both your immediate needs and your long-term objectives, such as retirement. Credit scores range from 300 to 850 on this scale. In general, a score of 700 or more is regarded as excellent. You may look for assistance from a qualified financial counselor or assess your credit score on several websites.

3. Rate of Savings

The foundation of all financial objectives is savings. Goals, no matter how big or long-term they may be, can only be realized by diligent saving. Savings must come from a well planned budget and rigorous adherence to the established parameters. However, it is common to stray from the plan, which lowers savings and hence hits the savings rate.

The monthly amount you must set aside for investments, retirement, big-ticket items, etc. is known as your savings rate. Setting your financial objectives requires that you decide on a saving rate. For instance, if your retirement objective is to have X dollars, you must determine how much money you would need to save right now in order to reach that amount in the allotted period. To get this rate, take into account your income as of right now and deduct all of your costs to get an amount that you may put into savings. The saving rate for reaching the goal of X dollars may then be calculated by dividing this amount by your income. Your odds are greater the higher the rate. The most ideal saving rate is thought to be 15%. It's also critical to account for variables like inflation, extraordinary costs, etc. in your savings strategy.

Both discretionary and non-discretionary costs should be noted in this context. When making allowances for expenses, it's critical to account for all non-discretionary expenditures, including bills, food, petrol, mortgage, and other unavoidable necessities. To increase the savings rate, you must restrict all other discretionary expenses, such as eating out, shopping, vacation, etc. Furthermore, you could not have any savings at all if your entire income is just sufficient to cover non-discretionary costs. As a result, you won't be able to reach your financial goals. There is likely more room for savings if overall income is high enough to cover non-discretionary expenses and leave enough for discretionary expenditure. Living within means (LWM) is an indicator that may be used to determine this.

LWM is equal to income (after taxes) at disposal / non-discretionary costs.

The likelihood of saving money improves with increasing LWM. Over time, a growth in your LWM will demonstrate your success in reaching your financial objectives.

4. Cash Balances

Monitoring your cash levels is one of the most popular and simple ways to stay on top of your financial objectives. By all means, you should always have a positive cash flow, but real or passive income, not debt or loans, should be the sources of your cash balances. The money you get from your assets, such as interest and rental income, is known as passive income. This is the revenue you get as a result of your money increasing over time. You must add your passive income to your real income in order to get your monthly cash flow. However, you must first deduct your costs in order to determine your monthly cash balance. A healthy financial condition is shown by a positive number, and this has an effect on financial objectives.

To sum up

These four indicators will help you track your financial goals by generating a comprehensive scorecard that consistently shows your financial health. If you want to be more focused and dedicated to achieving your financial goals, try modifying your saving and spending practices in line with these indicators. By closely adhering to the execution strategy of your plan and frequently assessing it, you will ascertain if you are moving in the right path.

B. Adjusting Your Financial Plan as Needed

Achieving financial security takes constant work and attention to detail rather than a single effort. It's critical to keep an eye on your financial plan at all times, evaluate your progress, and make any required modifications as you go. The following are recommended reasons for keeping an eye on and modifying your financial plan:

1. One common saying is "what gets measured, gets managed." When it comes to keeping an eye on and tweaking your financial strategy, this proverb is accurate. A financial plan requires frequent check-ins and revisions to make sure you remain on track toward your objectives, just like any other plan. Monitoring and tweaking your financial plan entails keeping tabs on your progress, evaluating your financial status on a regular basis, and making the required adjustments to make your plan work as best it can.

Financial Makeover

2. Individuals should keep an eye on and make adjustments to their financial strategy for many reasons. First of all, things happen unexpectedly in life, and things could alter in your financial situation over time. By keeping an eye on your plan on a regular basis, you may see any weaknesses or places for development and adapt your strategy accordingly. For instance, you may wish to update your savings objectives or think about raising your investments if your income increases significantly. However, in the event of a financial setback, you may need to review your spending plan and look for methods to reduce costs or raise revenue.

3. Keeping an eye on your financial plan also keeps you motivated and goal-focused. By monitoring your progress, you may recognize and acknowledge your accomplishments along the way, which can give you a feeling of pride and inspire you to keep working toward your financial objectives. Furthermore, frequent observation enables you to see any possible barriers or impediments that can prevent you from moving forward. You may, for example, take proactive measures to manage your debt if you realize that it is not going down as rapidly as you had hoped. You might look into debt consolidation possibilities or get financial counsel.

The following actions will help you monitor and modify your financial plan:

- **Review your financial objectives:** Take the time to ensure that your financial objectives still align with your goals and current situation. Would you want to add any more goals to your list? Are there any goals that are no longer relevant? By periodically assessing your goals, you can ensure that your plan remains relevant and focused on your needs.

- **Track your progress:** Use available tools and resources to monitor how you're doing in relation to your financial goals. Keeping track of your income, expenses, debt, savings, and assets may fall under this category. Regularly going over these components can help you identify any areas that need improvement or change.

- **Assess your financial situation:** Look at your income, expenses, assets, and obligations to ascertain your current financial situation. For example, if you find that your expenses are consistently more than your income, you may need to reassess your budget and search for places where you can save money.

- **Seek expert guidance**: To obtain an unbiased opinion on your financial strategy, think about speaking with a financial counselor. A professional's knowledge and experience allow them to provide insightful advice and suggestions. They may direct you toward the finest possibilities for modifying your strategy, provide substitute tactics, and assist you in identifying any hazards.

- **Be adaptive and flexible:** Keep in mind that a financial strategy is subject to change. Because life is dynamic, your strategy should be flexible enough to adjust to new situations. Remain flexible and prepared to change course as necessary. Maintaining the efficacy and relevance of your financial strategy requires flexibility.

A crucial component of reaching your financial objectives is keeping an eye on and modifying your financial plan. You can remain on track and overcome any obstacles by routinely evaluating your strategy, monitoring your development, and making the required modifications. You may maximize your strategy and raise your chances of achieving your intended financial results by being proactive in keeping an eye on your financial plan.

C. Milestone Celebration: Honoring Your Successes Along the Way

It is a worthy accomplishment to reach a financial milestone. These events, which might include meeting a savings target, paying off a sizable debt, or hitting an investment portfolio milestone, not only signal advancement but also serve as a source of inspiration to keep moving forward toward financial success. Marking these achievements not only lets you treat yourself to a reward for your efforts, but it also lets you realize how much it has improved your financial situation overall.

Celebrating financial milestones has varied meanings and importance depending on one's perspective. It could represent a moment of relief and release from debt for certain people. For others, it can mean that their long-term financial objectives—like owning a home or retiring comfortably—are becoming closer. Whatever the exact objective, remembering to celebrate these accomplishments is a crucial step on the path to financial security and shouldn't be disregarded.

1. Evaluate your progress: When celebrating a financial achievement, pause to consider the path that brought you thus far. Consider the things you gave up, the adjustments you made to your spending patterns, and the perseverance you showed all along the way. Not only will acknowledging your work make you feel more confident about yourself, but it will also keep you motivated to pursue other financial goals.

2. Treat yourself within reason: Rewarding yourself when you meet a financial goal is vital, but it's also necessary to do so sensibly. Rather than going overboard with a lavish trip or luxury purchase, think about rewarding yourself with something that is within your budget. If you paid off a sizable amount of debt, for instance, you may celebrate by putting some of the money you had been using to pay down your debt toward saving for the future or creating an emergency fund.

3. Tell your loved ones about your accomplishments: Celebrating financial achievements with those you love and care about makes them much more special. By telling your loved ones and friends about your accomplishment, you encourage and inspire them to manage their money as well as fortify your network of support. To raise awareness of the value of having a healthy financial situation, think about throwing a little party or posting about your accomplishments on social media.

4. Establish new objectives: In order to keep moving forward on your path to financial success after reaching a financial milestone, you must establish new objectives. Without specific goals, it's easy to revert to old behaviors or lose track of your accomplishments. You keep up the pace and make sure you keep making wise financial decisions by establishing new objectives. For example, after paying off a credit card debt, your next objective would be to pay off your home or education loans to achieve debt freedom.

Chapter Seven

Living a Fulfilling Generous Life

A. Enjoying the Fruits of Your Financial Makeover: Living Debt-free and Stress-free

Imagine yourself on a lengthy, meandering road journey, and after many hours, you eventually begin to see the beautiful overlooks and jaw-dropping vistas you have been anticipating. That's similar to when your financial makeover reaches the stage where you can really begin to reap the rewards of your hard work. Reaching a savings goal or paying off debt completely aren't the main things; what matters is the sense of liberation and happiness that comes from knowing you're living the life you've always wanted.

Cherishing the Win-Winning Moments
Let's discuss those times when you become aware of how far you've come. Imagine a person similar to Jakes, who used to have a knot in his stomach whenever he opened a bill. He pays his expenses immediately, certain

that he will have enough money. He takes a minute to really process the fact that he is no longer in that terrified

state, maybe while holding a cup of coffee on a calm morning. He's made progress, and it feels amazing.

Rejoicing Without Excessive Joy
While it's important to celebrate, the goal shouldn't be to erase all of your hard work. Consider Jakes's decision to designate a milestone. Instead of spending money on anything ostentatious that would make him seem bad, he invites a few close friends around for a cooked supper. They raise a glass to his accomplishments. It demonstrates that you don't need to spend a lot of money to celebrate in a manner that feels luxurious. It's warm, heartfelt, and uncomplicated.

Exchanging the Abundance of Wisdom
Jakes shares his path with others for more reasons than self-gratification. He tells his narrative in the hopes that it would ignite a flame in someone else. Imagine him guiding a buddy through his app for budgeting or outlining his debt-reduction strategy. It's about hope, not simply financial advice. Furthermore, Jakes has a sense of delight and accomplishment that surpasses any personal achievement when his buddy begins to make significant financial progress.

Greater Ambition and Forward Planning

Now that the pressing issues have been resolved, Jakes is free to dream greater. Perhaps he's contemplating a vacation to Europe or launching a side project right now. These are the next mountains to climb, not simply daydreams. And now that he has the resources and self-assurance he needs, his goals don't seem as impossible. It seems exciting that they feel feasible.

Discovering Happiness in the Ordinary

But large aspirations aren't everything. Even Jakes finds fresh happiness in the little things in life. It's in the tranquility of a worry-free stroll through the park, in the giggles shared over coffee with friends, and in the little contributions he can now give to causes that inspire him. The trip to get here has added to the value of these moments, which are already treasured.

Reaping the rewards of your financial transformation is a very private matter. It's about taking a moment to acknowledge your success, celebrating in a manner that makes sense to you, sharing your story to encourage others, setting new goals, and finding happiness in both the major and little victories. It's about living a life that you've made secure and full of possibilities by your own perseverance and hard work.

B. Giving Back: Using Your Financial Resources to Make a Positive Impact

You find yourself at a significant turning point in your financial life when you realize that managing your resources with purpose and not simply scraping by is more important than merely making ends meet or paying off debt. At this point, you may begin to consider using your riches to change the world rather than just focusing on your own financial objectives. This transformation affects not only how you divide your finances but also how you see yourself and your role in the world.

Recognizing Your Ability to Participate

Regardless of the amount in our bank account, everyone of us has the ability to effect change. Imagine someone like Sarah, who finds herself in a position to give back after years of diligent saving and planning. Maybe she begins small, buying goods from firms that pay fair wages or patronizing nearby enterprises that boost the local economy. Using her financial resources to reflect her ideals and have a good influence starts with this.

Finding Causes That Affect You Importantly:

Sarah wants her donations to support causes that she finds personally meaningful. She takes some time to

think about the causes that are important to her, whether they be social justice, environmental preservation, education, or animal welfare. She then conducts her research to identify groups that share her beliefs. It goes beyond just writing checks to ensure that her money really impacts causes close to her heart.

Integrating Giving Into Your Budget
Sarah chooses to include philanthropy in her financial plan and allocates a certain portion of her earnings to charity contributions. Like savings and spending, this is a purposeful aspect of her budget; it wasn't made randomly. She views her donations as investments in her principles since she is aware that little changes may have a big impact over time.

Giving of Your Time and Expertise
Sarah is aware that having a good influence extends beyond financial gain. She searches for chances to provide her time and expertise to groups in need. Giving back to the community, whether it is by volunteering at a local organization, teaching young people in her area, or lending her marketing experience, Sarah discovers that time improves her life in ways that material wealth cannot.

Promoting Change

Beyond gifts of cash and volunteer work, Sarah raises her voice in support of the issues that are important to her. She is aware that systemic changes are often necessary for meaningful change and that her activism may have an impact on such changes. Sarah is aware that her active participation will have a significant impact on a broader movement for good change, whether it is via attending community meetings, advocating for legislation changes, or just teaching her classmates about the concerns.

Corresponding Effects

When one person makes the decision to use their financial resources for the greater good, it can spread like wildfire and encourage others to follow suit. As a result of her decisions, Sarah discovers that her friends and family are impacted, which starts discussions about morality, generosity, and community involvement. As her network starts to realize how their financial choices can benefit society as a whole, her journey becomes one that involves everyone.

Examining the Effect

Sarah considers the effects of her contributions from time to time. She notices improvement when she considers the causes she has championed, the organizations she has donated to, and her volunteer work. Her sense of fulfillment from being a part of a community striving for positive change is profound, even though it's not always measurable.

One of the most effective ways to expand your influence outside of your immediate circle is to use your financial resources to benefit others. Aligning your financial decisions with your values, supporting the causes that are important to you, and realizing that, in the end, your choices about how much money you spend, save, and donate can leave a legacy of positive change are all important aspects of this. For Sarah and all those who follow this route, the journey is about more than just accumulating wealth; it's about personal and societal development.

C. Money Myths You Should Disbelieve Right Now

Myths about money are incorrect ideas you may have about it. We have been indoctrinated or implanted with these incorrect assumptions by family members or acquaintances who have certain views toward money. Many of us, to our own disadvantage, carry about these false beliefs about money that society has taught us. These financial fallacies prevent us from reaching our financial independence and goal-setting as well as from being financially savvy. Your prospects of achieving financial success are harmed if you have ever looked at what others say about money and based significant financial choices on those falsehoods. Some of us choose to disregard these financial warning signs, even though the majority of us have no clue what these money fallacies even are. Having a healthier relationship with money requires financial literacy and dispelling some financial money fallacies.

Everybody hears the same financial advice growing up: save more, invest early, and spend less. While all of this advice on money management is accurate, others are just untrue. Here are eleven common financial fallacies that may be confusing people today.

Myth No.1: Credit is NEVER Better Than Debit
Although credit cards are often associated with debt accumulation, they really provide a lot of advantages. First off, a lot of credit cards come with benefits like cashback, gas savings, and other advantages. Second, having a solid credit history is essential to your overall financial health. Using credit cards, keeping your balances low, and making your monthly payments on time are simple ways to do this. Last but not least, a lot

of credit cards come with purchase protection, which makes using them as a payment option for expensive goods wise.

Myth No.2: Buy a House by all Means
Greater independence and flexibility are benefits of house ownership, but ownership also entails greater responsibility and upkeep expenditures. Renting may be a preferable option for a number of individuals, including those who want to travel around a lot, don't want to worry about the expense of house upkeep, or can't afford the higher upfront expenditures of buying.

Myth No.3: Only Wealthy People Invest
Investments can be made by everyone, even with little funds. Every objective has an alternative, whether it's in the stock market, a long-term IRA, or a short-term certificate account. Investing wisely might be the greatest way to get the most of your money and move toward financial freedom.

Myth No.4: Since my spouse handles the finances, I don't need to be financially knowledgeable
Regardless of the role their spouse plays in the family budget, every adult should be able to manage it. Although one person handling the family's finances actively is acceptable, it is important for both partners to be informed of the family's financial situation and to be

prepared to handle investments and household bills in case of emergency.

Myth No.5: I Can Handle Any Financial Crisis With Credit Cards

Using credit cards to help you through a difficult time financially is a certain way to wind yourself deeply in debt. Depending on your circumstances, you may not be able to pay off your credit cards on time. In addition, you can wind up paying a lot more in interest and late penalties than you originally paid. In the event of a true financial emergency—such as a job loss, divorce, or major illness—credit cards should never be depended upon. To ensure that you are ready for any unforeseen circumstances, it is advisable to proactively accumulate an emergency fund that is equivalent to three to six months' worth of living expenditures.

Myth No. 6: I'm Too Young to Consider Retiring

When it comes to time for you to retire, the earlier you start saving for retirement, the less you'll need to contribute each month. Make the most of your workplace contributions (if available) and maximize your 401(k) contributions to provide yourself a stress-free, happy retirement. You may start an IRA or explore for alternative higher-interest accounts if your workplace does not provide a retirement plan. Let compound interest do its magic starting now!

Myth No.7: I Don't Need to Budget Because I Have Enough Money

Not only those who live paycheck to paycheck should budget. Even those with six-figure incomes may quickly spend their way into debt if they don't have a reasonable budget in place. A budget can assist you in making wise financial decisions by making you examine how much you're spending on each area of your life (vehicle, home, subscriptions, etc.).

Myth No. 8: You can't purchase happiness with money.

To be honest, I find it really heartening that so many of us are gradually dispelling the fiction around money. It is false to believe that we cannot purchase pleasure with money. It isn't real. This is the reason why: Happiness is a sensation or emotion that results from appreciating good things in general, such comfort, or from being aware of one's own wellbeing. What can you purchase comfort with? Money. Thus, happiness may be purchased with money. Having money makes you feel good and provides those fleeting moments of joy that are the essence of pleasure. You are content if you can finally afford that dream home or vehicle, or if you can afford that pricey trip. But you have to put forth the effort to get an intrinsic sense of joy—a sense of fulfillment and contentment—inside of yourself. You should dispel the financial fallacy that says you can't purchase happiness with money now.

Myth No.9: A woman should never earn more money than her spouse
Although women's empowerment and equality continue to advance in society, most families and marriages still unfortunately reflect this reality. Couples that want to make significant financial choices together nevertheless get into arguments about whether or not a woman should make more money than her partner. It doesn't imply that a woman who earns more than a guy does not value or seek to undermine his contributions. This story has been handed down by society to several generations, and it is completely illogical. You both need to realize that if one of you can increase your income and lead a more comfortable lifestyle, it's okay. Retaining this money myth just serves to highlight how non-advanced and backwards you are in your quest for financial understanding.

Myth No.10: Having student debt is a positive thing
Because they offer favorable tax advantages and low interest rates, student loans are considered to be a

healthy kind of debt. It's a myth. Debt is annoying and bad for your ability to succeed financially. When you incur debt, you find that you are spending most of your time paying it off rather than making investments in

assets that will provide income over the long run. Avoid this trend if you're a student and you can get by on campus without taking out student loans. Students often want to overspend and spend this money on parties without considering the long-term financial effects.

Myth No.11: Creating money requires money.
There's a half truth to this money myth. To generate revenue, you don't necessarily have to actively invest your money. There are several "free" methods for earning money. You may use your love for writing or persuading, for instance, to your advantage and earn money doing so. But, if you want to step into business, you would need to be prepared and willing to commit capital. It's time to dispel the misconception that you need money in order to be successful.

Financial Makeover

Conclusion

As we come to an end in "Financial Makeover," let's take a moment to consider the land we've traveled together. We've traveled the whole personal financial landscape, from the rocky pathways of investing and saving to the gentle slopes of debt relief. We've successfully managed the difficulties of creating a budget, the complexities of financial planning, and the gratification that comes from reaching our financial objectives. Now that a new chapter in our financial life is about to begin, let's pause to reflect on what we've learned so far and map out our future.

The Trip: A Contemplation

Our quest to financial transformation was never about short cuts or easy ways to become rich. It was about building a strong foundation, piece by piece, for a day when our goals and objectives would not be overshadowed by financial concerns. We began by evaluating our financial situation, identifying our areas of strength, and admitting where we needed improvement. Then, we determined how to get there by setting attainable objectives and creating a plan of action. All the while, we developed our financial decision-making skills.

The Knowledge Acquired

One of the most important things we've learned is that financial wellness is a journey rather than a goal. It calls for perseverance, self-control, and a dedication to lifelong learning. As we've seen, creating a budget is not about constraint but rather about making deliberate decisions that support our objectives and ideals. We now know that having debt is really a difficulty that can be solved with determination and a well-thought-out strategy, not a life sentence. Perhaps most significantly, we've learned that anybody who is prepared to dedicate themselves to a path of financial caution and knowledge can achieve financial independence.

Looking Ahead: Your Financial Makeover's Future Prospects

As you go, keep in mind that your financial makeover is a customized path that is specific to you and your situation. The concepts and tactics we have discussed are weapons in your toolbox that you can customize and alter to suit your needs. Remain inquisitive, keep learning about money concerns, and be willing to modify your ideas if circumstances and the outside world change.

There will be detours and unforeseen twists on the road ahead. There will be changes in personal situations, economic climates, and financial ambitions. But with the information, abilities, and resilience you've acquired, you can handle these adjustments with poise and assurance.

Accepting a Financial Empowerment Future

Imagine a day in the future when you will have enough money to support your aspirations rather than being a cause of concern. A time in the future when you are free to make decisions that improve both your life and the lives of others around you. Transforming your relationship with money to enable you live your best life is the actual core of a financial makeover.

An Appeal for Intervention

I extend an invitation to you to embark on this financial journey with hope and excitement. Spread the word about your expertise, since empowering others financially is a gift that goes on giving. Furthermore, keep in mind that each action you take will get you one step closer to realizing your goal of financial well-being.

In conclusion, the goal of writing "Financial Makeover" was to provide you with a compass that would lead you to financial contentment and independence. Know that this chapter ends and a brand-new, exciting chapter in your financial path begins as you shut this book. Every day and every choice you make will determine how your finances turn out.

I am grateful that you let me share in your adventure. Cheers to more of your success in the future and making your financial goals a reality rather than just a pipe dream. Recall that the goal of your financial makeover is to create a life that is abundant, joyful, and purposeful—not just about the money.

Request for a Review

Dear Reader,

First of all, I would like to thank you for reading "Financial Makeover". I hope that reading its pages is both enlightening and empowering, guiding you toward a more stable financial future. I appreciate your feedback on the book and believe that potential readers would find your guidance to be equally valuable in assisting them in achieving financial stability.

Would you please take a few minutes to talk about your thoughts and experiences with "Financial Makeover"? Whether it inspired a financial makeover, changed someone's viewpoint, or offered consolation during hard financial circumstances, your advice is a priceless resource for anybody who may be seeking something similar.

The Importance of Your Review:

Advice for Others: Your review might serve as a guide for potential readers by showing them how "Financial Makeover" could be related to their own financial situations.

Assist the Writer: Your review will be incredibly helpful to the author, as it will encourage and inspire him to continue writing compelling contents.

Enhance Future Editions: Your recommendations will be very beneficial to future editions so that the book may continue to satisfy the audience's evolving needs.

How to Submit Your Review:

You may post your review with ease on Amazon or any other website where books are read and reviewed.

Writing Your Review:

When writing your review, keep the following points in mind:

- Which "Financial Makeover" element did you find most helpful?
- How has the book altered your approach to managing or organizing your finances?
- What advice would you provide others about "Financial Makeover"?

I really appreciate your consideration in reviewing "Financial Makeover". Your voice is crucial to the continued development and dissemination of the book, in addition to providing value to the public. I'm grateful for your assistance and important part in this journey.

Warm regards,
Derrick C. Porter

References

1. https://us.etrade.com/knowledge/library/getting started/prioritizing -financial goals/

2. www.merrilledge.com
   article>what-to-do-if-you-are-managing and prioritizing multiple financial goals-Merrill Edge

3. https://www.m/.com/articles/what-to-do-if-you-have-many-competing-financial-goals.html

4. Investment Planning/Hills Bank
   https://www.hillsbank.com/investment-planning.

www.ingramcontent.com/pod-product-compliance
Lightning Source LLC
Chambersburg PA
CBHW052204220526
45471CB00004B/1808